THE COMPLETE
QUILTING
COURSE

THE COMPLETE
QUILTING
COURSE

GAIL LAWTHER

NEW
BURLINGTON
BOOKS

A QUARTO BOOK

Published in 1997 by
New Burlington Books
6 Blundell Street
London N7 9BH

ISBN 1-86155-240-8

This book was designed and produced by
Quarto Publishing plc
6 Blundell Street
London N7 9BH

Senior Editor: Honor Head
Editor: Michelle Clark
Photography: Paul Forrester
Illustrations: Sharon Smith

Art Director: Moira Clinch
Assistant Art Director: Debbie Sumner
Publishing Director: Janet Slingsby

Typeset by the Brightside Partnership, London
Manufactured in Hong Kong by Regent Publishing Services Ltd.
Printed by Star Standard Industries, Singapore

CONTENTS

GETTING STARTED

A GREAT BONUS OF QUILTING IS THAT YOU NEED VERY
LITTLE SPECIAL EQUIPMENT TO PRODUCE IMPRESSIVE
RESULTS. FOR VERY COMPLICATED PATTERNS YOU CAN
BUY SPECIALLY MARKED TEMPLATES AND RULERS TO
MAKE THE JOB EASIER, BUT MOST QUILTING PATTERNS
CAN BE DRAWN AND MARKED ON THE FABRIC WITH
ORDINARY DRAWING EQUIPMENT, AND STITCHED WITH
THE NEEDLES, THREADS, AND FABRICS THAT YOU
ALREADY HAVE ON HAND.

MATERIALS

The materials you can use for quilting are many and varied – in fact, you can quilt practically any material in one way or another! However, there are some fabrics, threads, and battings that are particularly useful, especially if you are a beginner, and using suitable materials for a given project will help you to make the most of your quilting skills. If you are new to quilting, begin your work with some of the standard materials, but don't be afraid to experiment; there is no limit to the beautiful and interesting effects that you can achieve by combining different quilting methods with the wide variety of fabrics and threads.

FABRICS

GENERAL-PURPOSE QUILTING FABRICS

The most popular fabrics for most types of quilting are fairly firm, closely woven ones that show quilted textures well without losing their own shape.

Cottons are probably the most popular fabrics – choose close-textured fabrics such as dress cottons, poplins, and polished cottons. Polyester-cotton blends can be useful, but they look and behave slightly differently from pure cotton fabrics, so try not to mix the two types of fabric in the same project unless you want to exploit their differences.

Silk is wonderful for quilting, but can be a bit slippery, so baste it firmly in place. Slubbed, habutai, dress-weight, and crêpe de Chine silks are good choices.

Linen, upholstery-weight cotton, and closely woven wools are good if you want a thicker fabric for quilting.

Satins, synthetic fabrics, metallic fabrics, and materials such as suede and fine leather can all be used in different ways.

If you are making a project that will be washed, make sure that you choose washable materials throughout, for some fabrics shrink when washed the first time. It's a good precaution to wash them before you cut or stitch them to prevent any possible problems later.

For backing projects, either use the same fabric as you use for the top or choose a less expensive version of a similar fabric, and remember to use firm fabrics to back trapunto quilting.

FABRICS FOR SHADOW QUILTING

Many different sheer and translucent fabrics can be used for shadow quilting – organdy, organza, net, muslin, cheesecloth, voile, chiffon, fine lawn, etc.

They don't always have to be white, either; colored stuffings under pastel or medium-toned fabrics can produce some interesting visual effects. Some lining and interlining materials are also intriguing to experiment with.

FABRICS FOR APPLIQUÉ

Virtually any fabric can be used for appliqué – from the sheerest chiffon to the thickest corduroy or brocade. Often the texture and thickness of the fabric add an extra dimension to the work. Sometimes, too, the printed or woven patterns of the fabric suggest uses. For example, basketweave textures can be used to represent fences, or striped fabrics can be used to represent awnings or deckchairs.

BATTINGS

NATURAL FIBERS

In the past, cotton batting was the material normally used to pad quilts. Its relatively flat texture is well suited to detailed stitching; however, the fibers tend to pull apart easily, so that the lines of quilting must be quite close together to minimize this – no farther apart than 2 in (5 cm). Today it is possible to buy batting made of 80 percent cotton and 20 percent polyester, which has the feel and texture of pure cotton with some of the stability of polyester, which also makes it safe to wash (by hand), unlike pure cotton batting.

Wool batting is a warm and luxurious filling and, like cotton, lends itself to fine quilting stitches. It is relatively expensive, but may well be worth the cost for a special quilt.

Some wool batting is covered with a layer of cheesecloth or other thin fabric to reduce fiber migration. If your local quilting shop does not stock wool batting, you can get it by mail order.

Just a small selection of the many fabrics suitable for quilting. Firm cottons are ideal for many projects; while silks, satins, and metallic fabrics produce their own effects. Small patterns lend themselves well to patchwork; larger patterns and stripes work well with contour quilting.

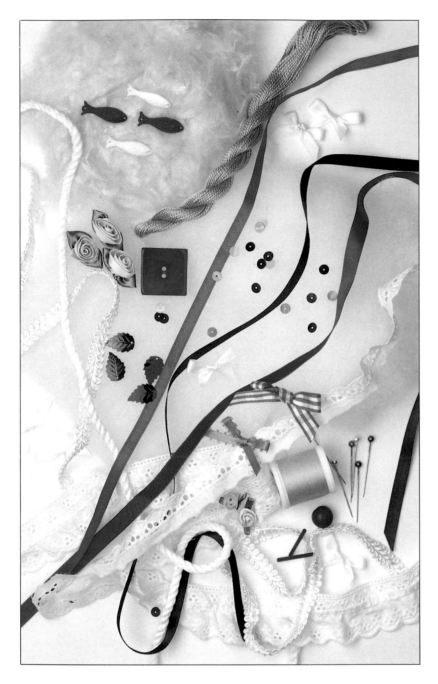

Braid, ribbon, and eyelet lace can provide the perfect finishing touches to your quilting. Sequins, buttons, beads, bows, and ribbon roses look very pretty when they're used for tied quilting, and cords of different thicknesses provide the texture in corded quilting.

SYNTHETIC FIBERS

The most popular batting is made from polyester, which has been felted and fluffed to form a springy, airy layer. It is strong and can withstand many washings. You can buy it in a variety of thicknesses – the degree of thickness being referred to as "loft": thus "low loft," "high loft," and so on. It is often finished with "bonding," a light glaze applied to both sides, to prevent the fibers from creeping through the top fabric (called "bearding").

Some polyester batting is treated with a process called "needlepunching". This entangles the fibers to produce a dense texture similar to that of cotton batting.

STUFFING

For trapunto quilting you will need polyester fiberfill. Or you can use fibers teased out of batting, or some absorbent cotton, which is less springy than polyester stuffing.

Some cotton stuffings are available, but they can be prone to the same problem. Polyester stuffing is light and washable, but can give a slightly coarser texture than the natural fibres.

THREADS

THREADS FOR HAND QUILTING

If you are quilting by hand, you can buy especially strong cotton-covered polyester quilting thread in a wide variety of colors. Heavy-duty mercerized cotton is also useful.

Ordinary sewing threads, silks, embroidery threads, and metallic threads can be used for small amounts of quilting or in short lengths; they tend to wear through and break more easily than quilting thread.

THREADS FOR MACHINE QUILTING

Ordinary sewing threads are fine for straight quilting by machine, but if you want to use one of the thicker embroidery threads, check that your machine is suitable and your needle is big enough.

Special machine embroidery threads are ideal for satin stitch or close zigzag appliqué work, etc., and many of the metallic threads on the market can be used in machines too, so long as you use a suitably-sized needle. An alternative is to use the thick thread in the bobbin and quilt with the right side underneath.

Transparent threads are available in two shades: a totally clear version for pale fabrics, and a smoke-colored version for dark fabrics. These can be useful when you want the texture of quilting but don't want the stitches themselves to stand out.

EXTRA MATERIALS

In addition to the materials listed, from time to time you will want other specialist items that will make your quilting work easier. You may find it useful, for example, to keep a stock of interfacing (stiffening material) in different weights (both iron-on and sew-in); transfer fusing web, used for fusing one material to another; and Stitch 'n' Tear, a special papery fabric used to give temporary support.

Other items you might need occasionally, or for particular techniques include stuffings for shadow quilting, bias binding, lace – including eyelet lace – ribbon, beads, sequins, buttons, cords for corded quilting, and so on, but these can be bought as you require them.

EQUIPMENT

The special equipment needed for quilting is minimal. Frames are useful, for example, but you will find that you can quilt small items perfectly well without one.

You will probably have most of the equipment you need in your sewing box already, but you may want to invest in a few inexpensive items that will make your quilting easier, such as a water-soluble pen or a pack of dressmaker's carbon paper.

Other specialized items, such as quilting stencils, can be bought as you need them.

GENERAL SEWING EQUIPMENT

NEEDLES

Ordinary sharps and crewels are useful for most types of quilting, but some quilters prefer short betweens needles, which are more maneuverable. Straw and milliner's needles are extra-long and so they are better for basting than for quilting proper.

Blunt-ended needles such as tapestry needles can be used for marking fabric (they make a faint indentation in the weave), and large-eyed needles and bodkins are very useful for threading the cords in corded quilting.

PINS

Ordinary glass-headed pins are fine for most jobs. However, you may want to buy some silk pins, which are extra fine, if you are working on silk, since they don't leave any marks on the fabric.

T-pins are useful when you are machine-stitching.

FRAMES

Quilting frames are available in two broad types: round and rectangular.

Round frames are like large embroidery hoops and can be hand-held or mounted on stands. They are used for stretching and stitching small projects or for quilting larger areas one bit at a time.

Rectangular frames are used for stretching larger quilts and can be flat or rolling: on flat frames, medium-sized projects can be stretched flat; on rolling

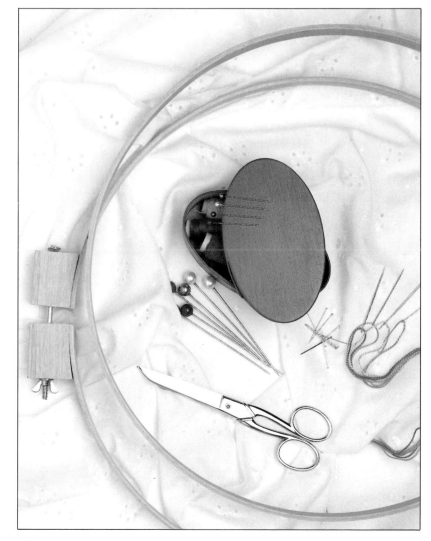

Keep a good selection of general-purpose sewing equipment, and you'll have most of the items needed for quilting. You'll need needles of different sizes for quilting, embroidering, and finishing projects, and sharp scissors for cutting out fabrics accurately. A quilting hoop is also useful to have.

frames the quilt is attached at both sides, then the area not being worked on is rolled onto the support at one side.

CUTTING EQUIPMENT

You will need a selection of scissors of different sizes: small, very sharp embroidery scissors with fine points for corded and trapunto quilting; ordinary small scissors for snipping threads; large scissors for cutting out fabric; and general-purpose scissors for cutting paper, templates, etc. You may also find that pinking shears are useful for finishing some seams.

One item you might consider buying, especially if you plan to do a lot of patchwork, is a rotary cutter and board. The cutter cuts through several layers of fabric at once and saves a great deal of time if you need to cut numerous shaped pattern pieces.

OTHER USEFUL SEWING EQUIPMENT

Many people find it impossible to quilt by hand without using a thimble – in fact some quilters use one thimble on each hand and sometimes one on the thumb, too!

A sewing machine is not necessary for all quilted projects, but many types of quilting can be adapted to machine stitching, and, of course, it is always useful for assembling items. Certain sewing machine accessories, such as twin needles, a cording foot and a quilter bar are very useful to the quilter.

You will need a tape measure, and you may find a "quilter's quarter" a handy piece of equipment. It is a long, straight piece of clear plastic, square in section, each side measuring ¼ in (6 mm), and is used for adding narrow seam allowances to patchwork and appliqué pieces.

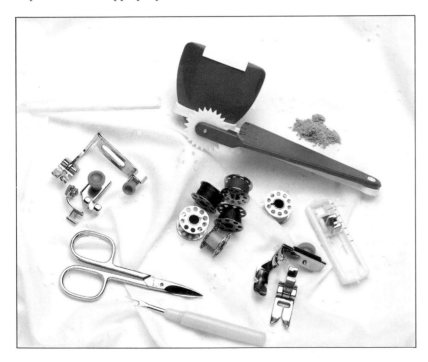

A few small pieces of specialized equipment will make your quilting go smoothly.

It's often important to draw up quilting and patchwork designs very accurately. As shown right, supplement ordinary drawing equipment with specialized graph paper and template plastic.

GENERAL DRAWING EQUIPMENT

EQUIPMENT FOR DESIGNING AND ENLARGING PATTERNS

Standard pencils, erasers, rulers, and drawing paper are used for drawing and tracing designs, but dressmaker's or ordinary graph paper is useful when enlarging them.

Quilting designs are often available as stencils, but if you want to make your own stencils, template plastic is ideal. Some firms also produce special graph boards or shaped templates (circles, diamonds, or triangles) marked with different divisions, which save a great deal of measuring and drawing when you are designing your own quilting or patchwork patterns.

EQUIPMENT FOR TRANSFERRING PATTERNS

There are many different ways of transferring patterns to your fabric, and the method will vary according to the pattern, the fabric, and whether or not the traced lines will be covered by the final stitching.

On pale fabrics, patterns can often be traced, either in soft pencil, if the lines will be covered, or in special water-soluble or fading pen. You can do this by laying the fabric over the design, which you have drawn over with black pen so it shows through the fabric, and tracing over the lines you can see; or you can tape the design and fabric to a window and trace the lines of the design beneath (the advantage of this latter method is that even fine lines are clearly visible as the light shines through the paper and fabric).

Water-soluble pen marks can be sponged away with a damp cloth when the stitching is complete, while fading pen marks gradually disappear – often within 24 hours, so don't mark a large area at a time in this way!

On dark fabrics you can use tailor's chalk. Dressmaker's carbon paper is available in various colors and is used in the same way as ordinary carbon paper. You lay the paper, carbon side down, on the right side of the fabric, then cover it with the paper holding your design and trace over the design with a pencil or blunt needle.

Tracing wheels are serrated wheels used with dressmaker's carbon. You lay your design over the fabric, with the carbon between the two, and run the tracing wheel over the lines. The serrations pierce the paper and leave a dotted line.

Traditional embroidery transfers are printed in reverse and then ironed onto your work, but they leave a dark line that will not wash out, so the stitching must be thick enough to cover the lines. Transfer pencils for drawing your own transfers of this kind are also available. Some commercially produced quilting transfers use a similar technique, but with silver lines, which show less but may still be visible after stitching.

OTHER EQUIPMENT

From time to time you will need other pieces of equipment to finish your quilting projects. These include glue, tape, double-sided basting tape (this holds small pieces of fabric in place instead of basting), craft knives, card blanks, etc. You will also need a good iron, as most of your fabrics should be pressed before use – do remember not to iron batting as it flattens it permanently.

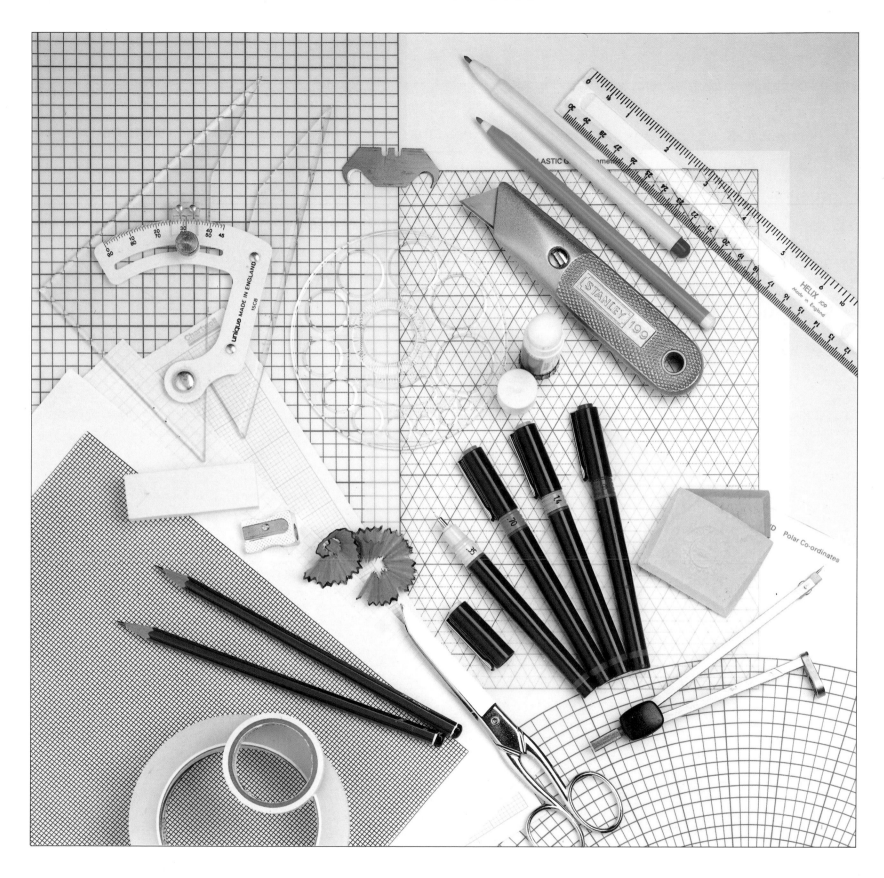

STITCHES

Although there are many stitches that can be used for quilting, including most outline stitches, many techniques use the same few basic ones. Hand quilting stitches are used most often to produce a texture in the padded layers, rather than as a decorative feature in themselves. These days, of course, it is possible to work many quilting techniques by machine as well as by hand. Don't think of machine quilting as a poor relation of hand quilting – it has its own strengths, and versatile modern machines can produce unique effects that are impossible to imitate by hand.

HAND QUILTING STITCHES

RUNNING STITCH

This is the most basic of all stitches and is the traditional stitch used when doing traditional quilting by hand. It can also be used for many other techniques, such as contour quilting and random quilting. The needle is pushed in and out of the fabric in small, even stitches.

BACKSTITCH

Backstitch is excellent for producing the strong lines of stitching necessary for corded quilting and other techniques such as shadow quilting and trapunto where an unbroken stitching line is needed. The needle is put into the fabric at the tip of the preceding stitch, and emerges the same distance again along the stitching line.

CHAIN STITCH

Chain stitch can be used to provide a thicker, more decorative line than backstitch. The needle is brought to the front of the fabric then re-inserted at the same place, emerging farther along the stitching line so that it catches a loop of thread to make one link in the chain.

MACHINE QUILTING STITCHES

STRAIGHT STITCH

Straight stitch is ordinary machine stitching. It is used when you want a thin line of stitching that doesn't show too much, as in basic quilting or trapunto, and is also useful for quilting patchwork shapes.

SATIN STITCH

If you don't have a satin stitch option on your machine, set it to the closest possible zigzag stitch, and that will have a similar effect. Use satin stitch for attaching the edges of appliqué shapes and for quilting thick colored bars.

ZIGZAG

Zigzag is useful for making unusual quilting lines and also for quilting appliqué shapes that have been attached with transfer fusing web so that they don't fray.

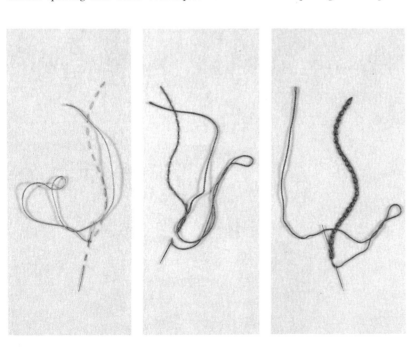

The three stitches you'll find most useful for quilting by hand are, from left to right, running stitch, backstitch and chain stitch.

As these examples show, both machine (right) and hand (left) quilting have been used to make up the projects in this book.

FINISHING TECHNIQUES

Finishing techniques may seem a strange item to have at the beginning of a book, but you need to bear in mind the way you will finish your project from the very earliest stages, since any borders, bindings, lattice strips, or ruffles will be an integral part of the finished design. The techniques shown here are some of the most popular finishing methods. Choose the one that you think will work best for each item that you quilt, and decide whether you will use a matching, harmonizing, or contrasting color.

STITCHES

Running stitch, backstitch, chain stitch.

Straight stitch, zigzag stitch, satin stitch.

STRAIGHT BINDING WITH STRIPS

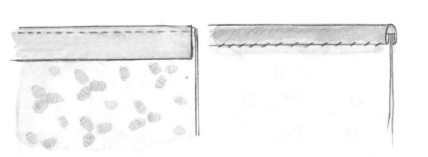

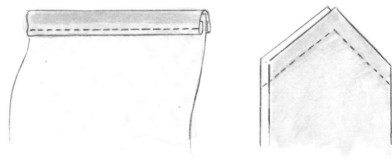

For invisible stitching, lay the strips of binding fabric on the quilt front, right sides together, and stitch by hand or machine along the seamline. Fold the binding over the quilt edge, turn under the seam allowance on the raw edge of the binding fabric, and slipstitch it neatly and invisibly to the backing fabric.

For one-seam straight binding, fold under both of the raw edges of the binding fabric and then fold the binding in half lengthwise. Slip the folded binding over the raw edges of the quilt, and baste near the folded edges so that both the front and the back edges of the binding are caught down, then stitch along this line by machine. For mitered corners on both sides, cut and stitch the binding strips in the shape shown before applying the binding to the quilt.

STRAIGHT BINDING WITH BACKING

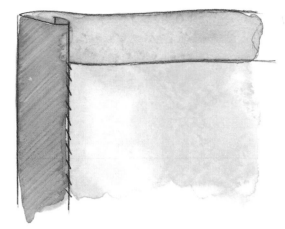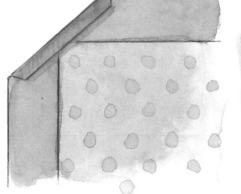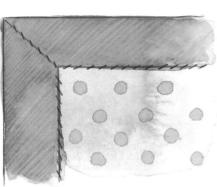

When binding with the backing fabric, make sure that your backing fabric is bigger than your top fabric. Press under the raw edge, then fold the fabric over the front of the quilt and stitch down by hand or by machine.

For mitered corners on the front, trim the backing fabric across the corner as shown, then turn under and slipstitch the diagonal edges together before you sew the rest of the binding in place.

BIAS BINDING

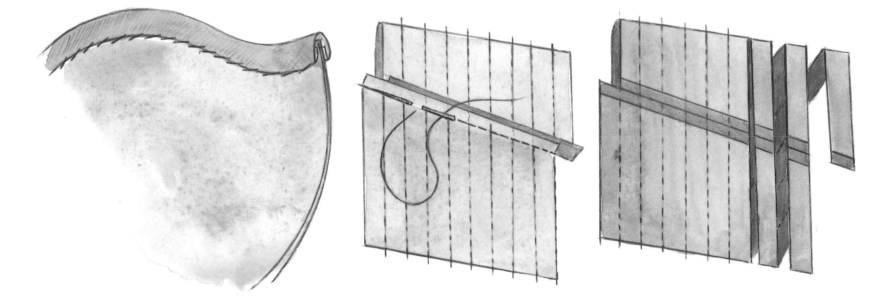

Purchased or made bias binding can be attached by hand or by machine in the same way as straight binding (the first two methods above), but has the advantage that it can be curved around corners, so it is useful for binding curves and irregular shapes.

To make your own bias binding, mark diagonal strips at regular intervals across a large rectangle of fabric as shown, then join the straight sides, aligning the raw edge with the first pencil line in from the end at each end. Starting at one end, cut along the line, and you'll find that you produce one long bias strip, which saves your having to join individual ones all the time.

LACE, EYELET LACE, AND RIBBON

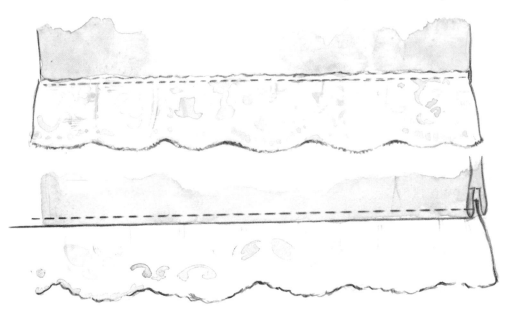

If the edge is neatly bound, you can simply attach it to the front of your hemmed quilt with slipstitches or machine stitching.

If you want to hide raw edges or gathers or prefer to finish your quilt edges at the same time, press under the raw edges of the quilt and backing, baste the edging in between, and then stitch just inside the edge by hand or machine.

For invisible insertion, stitch the edging to the front of the quilt first, aligning the edge of the edging with the edge of the quilt so that the decorative edge is toward the center. Then turn the raw edge under to the back, press, and slipstitch the backing fabric to the underside of the edging.

RUFFLES

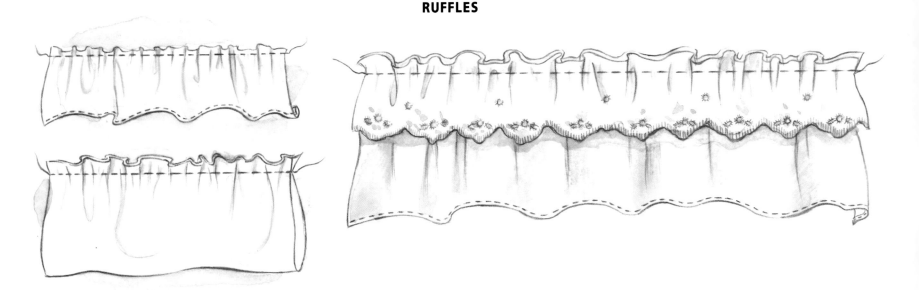

For a single ruffle, turn a narrow double hem under along a gathered strip of fabric, and sew it in place by hand, by machine straight stitch, or by machine blind hemming. Insert using either the second or third method given in the lace and ribbon section, above.

For a folded ruffle, fold a wider strip of fabric in half lengthwise, and gather it along

the aligned raw edges, then insert using either the second or third method given in the lace and ribbon section above.

For a double ruffle, make two fabric ruffles of different widths, or make one of fabric and one of lace, eyelet lace, or ribbon, gather them together and insert using either the second or third method given in the lace, eyelet lace, and ribbon section, above.

CORDING

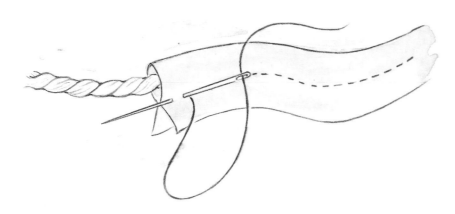

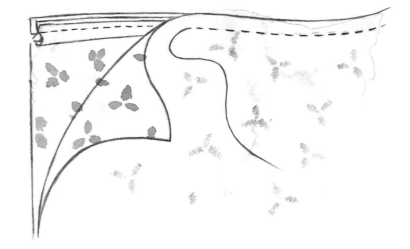

If you want to cord the edge of your quilt, cut a strip of bias binding the same measurement as the circumference. (If you are cording a straight edge, the fabric doesn't need to be on the bias.) Fold it over filler cord, and stitch the two layers of

fabric together by hand or machine, as close to the cord as possible. Insert this seam between the front and back of the quilt so that the covered cord lies along the finished edge of the quilt, raw edges together.

PLAIN HEMS

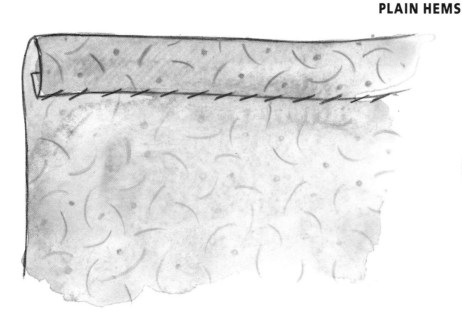

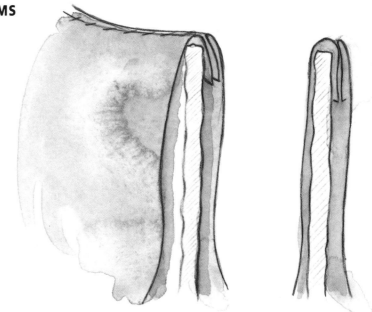

For a turned hem, press under a double hem to the wrong side along the raw edges, and stitch it in place on the wrong side using slipstitches or hand-hemming stitches, or machine stitching.

For hems on bulkier items, when you don't want to use a double hem on the raw edges, turn the edges of the front and the backing in toward the batting, folding one of the edges over the batting so that it is concealed. Stitch the two layers together by machine, or slipstitch or oversew the folds together.

THE PROJECTS

Generally, the projects are arranged from the easiest technique to the more difficult, but each has full instructions, so as soon as you've mastered the basic principles of quilting you should be able to produce any of the items featured. Tip boxes and notes on how to adapt the featured project insure that you achieve a professional result to suit your specific requirement. In this section you'll also find inspirational items that will whet your appetite for taking each technique further in your own projects.

CHAPTER 1

CONTOUR QUILTING

Contour quilting is the simplest possible type of quilting – you don't even need to transfer a design onto your fabric, because you just stitch along the lines of a printed fabric. When you're selecting a fabric for contour quilting, choose one that has obvious bold shapes that you can quilt around: stripes, plaids, and bold, splashy patterns look very effective. Some quilting shops sell fabric panels specially printed with patterns that can be quilted and then made into pillows, crib quilts, or even garments, and these make very good starter pieces if you are new to quilting. Contour quilting can be done by machine or by hand. If you are quilting by machine, use an ordinary straight stitch; if you are stitching by hand, use running stitch or backstitch.

+ + + **CONTOUR QUILTING · PROJECT 1** + + +

CRIB QUILT

This pretty crib quilt uses a pre-printed fabric panel. These are available in various nursery designs. Alternatively you could use an all-over print, provided that the main motifs are good sized. The same print, or a related solid color, could be used for curtains and pillows.

Pre-gathered eyelet lace has been used to finish the edge of this quilt, but if you prefer, you could make a ruffle or a binding in a fabric that matches your chosen panel design.

Preparation
Check that the edges of the printed panel have been cut straight and that any border pattern is the same width on both sides of the panel.

Wash and press the panel and the backing fabric.

Quilting
1 Spread the backing fabric right side down on a flat surface, and position the batting on top of it, leaving an even border all around. Place the printed panel, right side up, on top of the batting and pin the three layers together at intervals, working from the center out in each direction. Baste through all three layers at regular intervals across the width of the quilt, and then remove the pins.
2 Choose the main lines of the design as your quilting guides, and baste about 1 in (2.5 cm) away from each line, following the shapes.
3 If you are quilting by machine, stitch along the main lines of the design, using a medium-length straight stitch, changing direction carefully at corners and around any irregular shapes so as not to twist or bunch up the fabric. Finish off

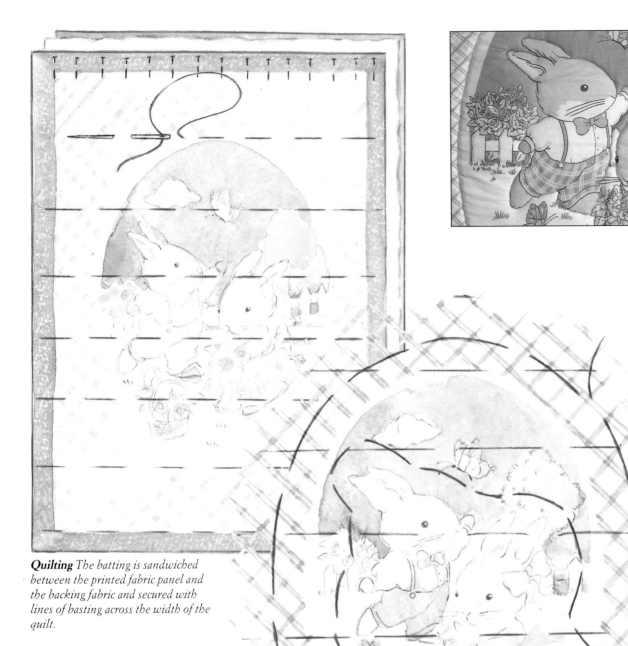

Quilting *The batting is sandwiched between the printed fabric panel and the backing fabric and secured with lines of basting across the width of the quilt.*

Lines of basting are worked around each main line of the printed pattern, about 1 in (2.5 cm) outside the lines.

the threads firmly at the end of every stitching line, either by working back and forth for a few stitches or by pulling the threads through to the back and knotting them. Remove the basting threads.

If you are quilting by hand, stitch around the main lines of the design using small, even running stitches. Remove the basting threads.

Finishing

4 Press 1 in (2.5 cm) to the wrong side around the edges of the printed panel and also around the edges of the backing fabric.

5 Baste the two layers of fabric together, sandwiching the eyelet lace between them (make sure that the eyelet lace is right side up when seen from the front). Pleat the eyelet lace at each of the corners, to make sure that it doesn't pull.

6 Run a line of straight machine stitching around the edges of the quilt, fastening the front to the back and the eyelet lace in between, then remove the basting threads.

Variations

This very simple method of quilting can be used for bigger projects, too: choose printed sheeting in a pattern that matches your bedroom curtains or carpet to make a quilt for your own room; use a length of a children's print to make a unique throw-over cover to brighten up a child's room; buy square printed panels and quilt them in the same way to make pillow covers. Many of them are based on patchwork patterns.

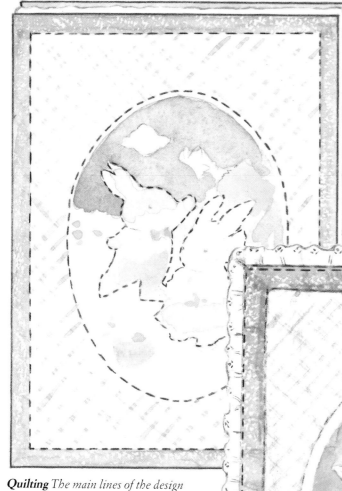

Quilting *The main lines of the design are quilted along by machine or hand and the basting threads removed.*

Finishing *The raw edges of the front panel and the backing fabric are pressed inward and the eyelet lace stitched in between them. The basting threads are then removed.*

TIPS FOR PROFESSIONAL RESULTS WHEN QUILTING BY HAND

● If you are quilting by hand, your stitches don't have to be especially short to look neat – just make them as even in length as possible.

● If you are using running stitch, select a long needle so that you can make several stitches with one pulling through of the thread. This makes the thread last longer without wearing through, as well as being quicker to work.

● For hand quilting, use either quilting thread or cotton-covered polyester sewing thread run over beeswax – it will be less likely to tangle.

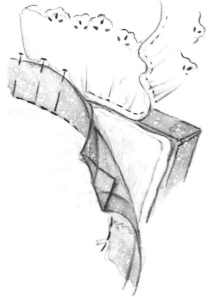

CONTOUR QUILTING · PROJECT 2

PLACEMATS

Use contour quilting to make a unique set of placemats for your dining room. Choose a fabric that matches or complements your decor – perhaps the same fabric as your draperies or upholstery – and cut out sections that you can then quilt and bind. All the mats can be the same, or you can quilt different sections of the pattern for each mat.

Preparation

Wash and press the top and backing fabrics.

Enlarge (see right) the mat pattern onto stiff paper and cut it out to make a template.

Quilting The mat shape is marked on the fabric, insuring that the chosen motifs are arranged as desired in the right positions.

The fabric is cut ⅜ in (1 cm) outside the marked line, leaving the pencil line as a stitching guide for the bias binding.

Quilting

1 Choose the shapes on the fabric design that you want to appear on the finished mat. Lay the fabric right side up on a flat surface, and position the template on the fabric so that the shapes fall where required. Use a soft pencil to draw around the edge of the template.

2 Cut around the mat shape, ⅜ in (1 cm) outside the pencil line. (The pencil line will act as your stitching guide for the seamline when it is time to attach the binding.)

3 Cut the backing fabric and the batting to the same shape as the patterned fabric.

4 Place the backing fabric right side down on a flat surface, position the batting on top, then lay the printed fabric, right side up, on top of the batting. Baste all three layers together with several lines of basting stitches in both directions.

5 If you are quilting by machine, stitch

The mat shape is basted to the batting and backing fabric, and the main lines of the design are stitched along by hand or by machine.

along the main lines of the design, using a medium-length straight stitch. Begin with the shapes nearest the center of the mat and work outward. Finish off the

1in
(2·5cm)

Pattern for the mat

Pattern for the placemat

TIPS FOR PROFESSIONAL RESULTS

• Always begin quilting the shapes nearest the center of the mat and work outward – this helps to prevent the fabric from puckering.

• Don't try to quilt every line on the fabric pattern, as this is very tedious; also, the impact of the quilted effect is then lost. Just choose a few bold shapes on each mat.

• If you can't find a fabric that matches your decor, choose a solid color and work random quilting on it (see page 54) or pick out the shape of a flower, say, from your printed fabric and stitch it on solid-colored fabric using the traditional quilting technique (see page 32).

• If your printed fabric is mostly dark in color, choose a dark bias binding for the edging; pale bindings can be rather see-through.

ends of each thread neatly and securely. If you are quilting by hand, quilt along the main lines of the fabric design using short, even running stitches. Begin with the shapes nearest the center of the mat and work outward.

Finishing

6 Remove the basting threads.
7 Finish the raw edges of the mat by stitching the bias binding over them, using the pencil line on the right side as a stitching guide. (See page 17 for methods of attaching bias binding.)

Variations

Once you have mastered the technique of contour quilting, there are numerous ways in which you can vary the details of a basic project. Here are three different versions of the contour quilted placemat. They have been done in the same shape as the mat in Project 2, but each variation here uses a different combination of fabric, thread, and stitching technique.

The opulence of a rich Oriental print is enhanced by the use of gold metallic thread used in running stitches along the main lines dividing different areas of the pattern. Because the print is asymmetrical, stitching these lines produces an attractive informal quilted design.

If you use metallic thread, thread your needle with a short length at a time; the thread tends to become frayed fairly easily, so longer lengths will be spoiled. The gold of the print and the thread is picked up again in the gold-colored satin bias binding, which has more sheen than cotton binding.

On the rainbow mat, the main lines of the motifs are stitched by hand, using running stitches sewn in white thread. The mat is edged in bright blue bias binding – picking up the blue in the rainbows and clouds – stitched on by machine in blue straight stitches so that the stitching doesn't stand out.

This placemat is made from striped fabric. The mat has been cut so that the main line of the pattern is in the center (with this kind of pattern the positioning of the template on the fabric is important if the mats are not to look asymmetrical). So-called "invisible" thread has been used to work rows of

machine zigzag stitching along and between selected stripes (don't be tempted to stitch too many of the stripes or you will lose the effect of the quilting). The bias binding, in a harmonizing fabric, is stitched in the same way; the zigzag stitch attaches the binding very securely.

*I*NSPIRATION

The beautiful printed fabrics available today can be used to produce very dramatic effects with contour quilting, but you don't have to limit yourself to using prints. Several of the examples here use designs that have been painted onto the fabric then quilted.

The resist method of silk painting – somewhat like batik – was used to produce the basic design for this jerkin. The dragon was painted first, then the rest of the fabric was dyed a deep rust orange. The dragon and stylized flower were contour quilted in multicolored metallic thread, then the background was machine quilted in the same thread using a twin needle to produce double lines of wavy stitching.

The bow below was worked as a trial piece for decorating a crib quilt. The design was stenciled onto the background with fabric paint, then contour quilted by hand over batting.

▼ *The delicate tones and shapes of the printed fabric on this pillow have been enhanced with contour quilting by hand, producing a soft and gentle effect.*

▲ *Printed fabric panels come in all shapes and sizes. This Christmas wreath was stitched from a pre-printed panel over thick batting, then quilted by machine along the straight lines of the design. The irregular border was bound with red bias binding.*

◄ *If you find patchwork a little daunting, cheat by using a pre-printed panel. On this pillow panel the lines of the stars and squares were contour quilted by machine before the pillow cover was assembled.*

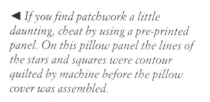

CHAPTER 2

TRADITIONAL QUILTING

In its most familiar form, quilting consists of three layers of fabric: a top fabric, a backing fabric, and a layer of soft padding sandwiched between them. The three layers are held together with lines of stitching worked in a decorative pattern. Many of these patterns originated in the British Isles and were brought to North America by colonists. These traditional designs include flower shapes, other natural forms such as feathers and leaves, and geometric and interweaving border and filling patterns. American quilters have often incorporated such motifs in patchwork, using them to embellish the solid areas within a quilt. The stitching is usually worked in thread matching the fabric, so that the stitches themselves are inconspicuous and the design is created by contrasting textures – although modern quilters are experimenting with variations on this tradition.

+ + + **TRADITIONAL QUILTING · PROJECT 1** + + +

NAUTILUS TEA COZY

White-on-white is a very elegant color scheme, and it complements the clean lines of this nautilus shell design perfectly. With no extra patterns to distract attention from the shape, the beautiful curves of the shell flow into one another.

You can either work the quilting on the front of the tea cozy and leave the back plain or reverse the image for the back so that the shell curves in the same direction on both sides.

Preparation

Enlarge the chart to the correct size, using the grid method (see page 26). This design gives a tea cozy 16 in (42 cm)

wide, but if you want a slightly bigger or smaller one, adjust your chart size and the amounts of fabric and batting accordingly.

Press the polished cotton pieces and the muslin.

Quilting

1 Mark the pattern on the right side of one of the white cotton fabric pieces with the water-soluble pen (see page 12).

2 Place one of the pieces of muslin on a flat surface, and cover it with one of the pieces of batting; place the marked fabric, right side up, on top of the

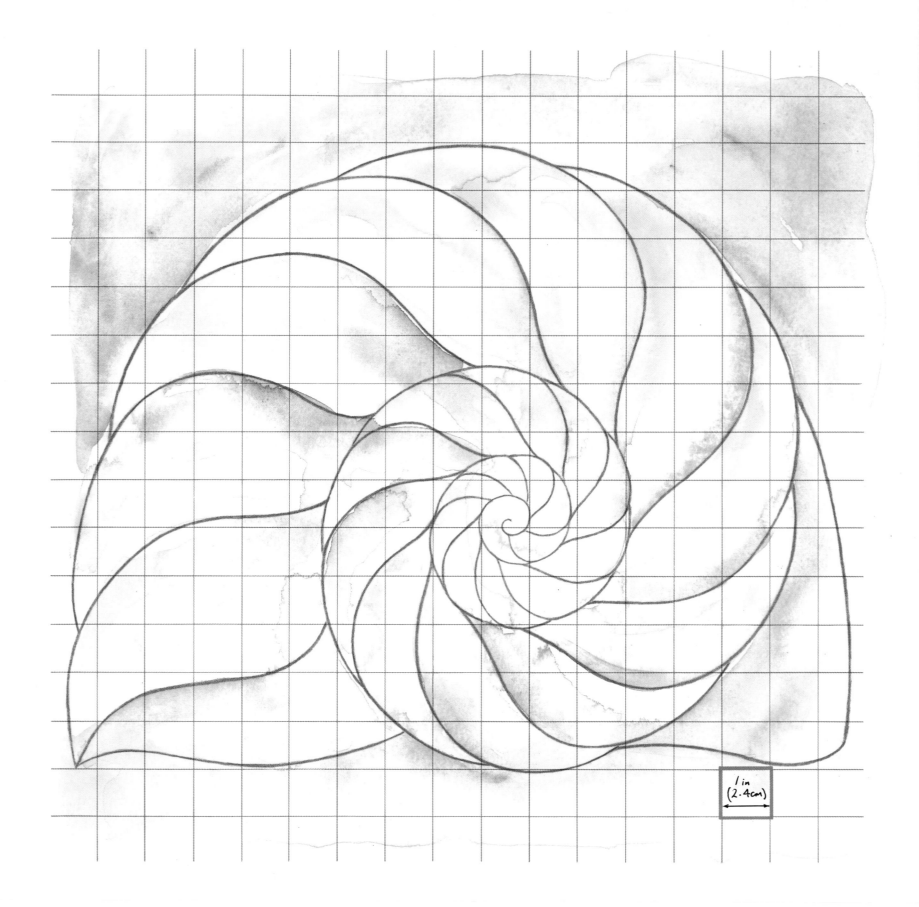

1 in
(2.4cm)

Pattern for the nautilus design

batting. Baste the three layers together in a spiral of basting stitches from the center outward.

3 Beginning in the center of the design, quilt the shape along the marked lines.

If you are quilting by machine, use a very slow speed and short, straight stitches for the very center of the design, turning the fabric very carefully to follow the curves exactly. Increase to a medium-length straight stitch as you reach the second spiral of the design. Finish off each line of stitching neatly and securely at both ends.

If you are quilting by hand, quilt along the marked lines in small, even running stitches or backstitches.

Finishing

4 Remove the basting threads, and lightly sponge away any pen marks with a clean damp cloth.

5 If you are stitching a shell on the other side of the tea cozy, reverse the image and repeat steps 1–4 on the other piece of white cotton. If you want the back of

the tea cozy to be plain, simply baste together the white cotton, batting, and muslin pieces.

6 Trim the front of the tea cozy so that you have an even curve around the top edge of the shell, 2 in (5 cm) from the stitching line. Lay the front and the back pieces together with right sides facing, and trim the back to the same shape. Trim the remaining two pieces of white cotton fabric to the same shape.

7 With right sides together, pin, baste, and machine stitch the front to the back along the curved edge, 1 in (2.5 cm) in from the edge. Trim the seam and turn the tea cozy right side out.

8 Put the other two pieces of white cotton together with right sides facing, and stitch a 1 in (2.5 cm) seam from the base to about 6 in (15 cm) up each side of the curve.

9 Slip this lining over the tea cozy, right sides together. Pin, baste, and machine stitch the straight seam along the base of the tea cozy, then turn it right side out through the gap in the lining seam.

10 Neatly slipstitch the gap in the lining seam closed, tucking the lining in to the inside of the tea cozy as you do so.

Variations

Although the nautilus design is perfectly suited to a tea cozy shape, you could also quilt it on a pillow cover or in the center of several blocks for a quilt, or team it up with a border of other shell shapes such as clams or whelks.

If you don't want to stitch the design in white on white, choose another pastel or a bright color, and quilt it in matching thread, or choose a fabric that has a very tiny print, one that won't detract from the curves of the shell.

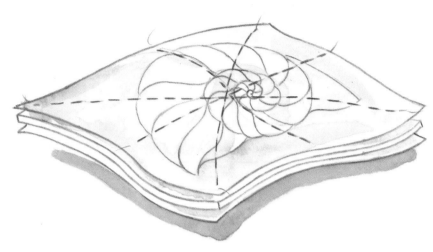

Quilting *The design is traced onto one piece of the white cotton using a water-soluble pen. The batting is sandwiched between the white cotton and the muslin.*

Quilting and finishing *The main lines of the design are quilted by hand or by machine; the pen lines will have already begun to fade, and any remaining marks are removed with a damp cloth.*

TIPS FOR PROFESSIONAL RESULTS

- If you are quilting by hand, your thread will remain free of tangles if you run it lightly across a lump of beeswax; but don't give it too heavy a coating or you will discolor the thread.

- Start quilting from the middle of the design outward; this will prevent the fabric from puckering as you work your way around the spiral.

- For extra elegance, insert cording into the curved seam of the tea cozy (see page 19).

TRADITIONAL QUILTING · PROJECT 2

*C*LASSIC PILLOW COVERS

These two pillow covers have been quilted in pretty pastels, using updated versions of traditional designs. The pink pillow design features a central rose motif, surrounded by a wavy Celtic-inspired border which twists and untwists over itself. The green pillow design has a central Celtic knot and is surrounded by a border of feathers – very common quilting motifs. The background of the green pillow cover has been given an overall texture with a checkered pattern. Such filling patterns are often used in traditional quilting to enhance and provide a contrast to the larger, more intricate patterns of the main motifs.

Preparation

Press the polished cotton and muslin squares.

Enlarge (see page 26) the patterns onto large sheets of paper (see page 12).

Mark pattern A on the right side of the pink cotton square and pattern B on the right side of the green square.

Quilting

1 Lay the squares of muslin side by side on a flat surface, cover with the squares of batting and lay the marked squares right side up on top of the batting. Baste all three layers together in a criss-cross pattern.

2 If you are quilting by machine, stitch along the lines of the designs with straight stitches, using matching thread.

If you are quilting by hand, quilt along the lines of the designs with small, even running stitches, using matching thread.

3 Remove the basting threads.

MATERIALS

1 square of polished cotton in rose pink, 20 in (50 cm) square
1 square of polished cotton in green, the same size as the pink cotton
2 squares of muslin, or other fine fabric, the same size as the pink cotton
2 squares of low loft polyester batting the same size as the pink cotton
2 backing panels of the pink cotton, each 12 x 18 in (30 x 45 cm)
2 backing panels of the green cotton, each same size as the pink panels
Quilting thread to match the green and pink fabrics
2 pillow forms, each 16 in (40 cm) square
Extra green and pink fabric and filler cord (optional) (see page 19)

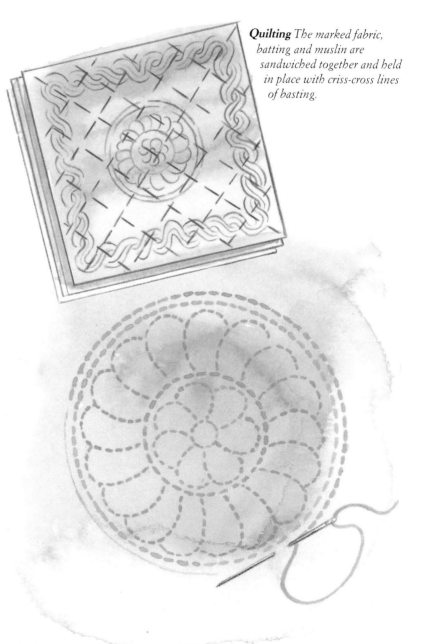

Quilting The marked fabric, batting and muslin are sandwiched together and held in place with criss-cross lines of basting.

The lines of the design are quilted using matching thread and either straight machine or small running stitches, then the basting threads are removed.

16in
(41cm)

Pattern A

15½in
(40cm)

Pattern B

Finishing The quilted fabric is trimmed to shape· on the pink pillow front, the corners are rounded off.

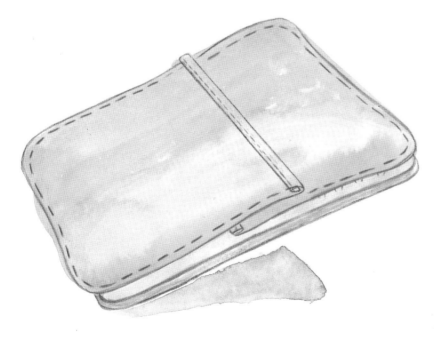

The backing panels are hemmed, each along one edge, then stitched to the pillow fronts, right sides together, hemmed edges overlapping.

TIPS FOR PROFESSIONAL RESULTS

● Mark the designs on your fabrics in crayon, choosing a crayon one or two shades darker than your fabric, sharpened to a good point. The stitching will cover most of the marks, and the rest won't show, as they will disappear into the contours of the quilting.

● If you can't find quilting thread in the exact shade you want, use ordinary sewing thread and run it over a block of beeswax: this will darken it and prevent tangles.

Finishing

4 Trim the edges of the squares evenly so each measures 18 in (45 cm) square. Cut the corners of the pink pillow cover so that they are rounded.

5 If you are cording the edges, cut the bias strips from your matching fabrics; cover the filler cord, and stitch the cording in place around the edges of the quilted shapes (see page 19).

6 Press under and stitch a narrow double hem along one of the long edges of each of the backing panels. Trim the corners of the opposite long edges on the pink panels so that they match the corners of the quilted front of the pink square.

7 Place the quilted squares right side up on a flat surface, and lay the matching backing panels on top of them, right side down, aligning them with the edges of the squares with the hemmed edges overlapping. Pin and baste them in place along the seamlines.

8 Stitch twice around the raw edges of each square, taking a 1 in (2.5 cm) seam allowance.

9 Trim the seams and the corners of the pillows, cutting them on the diagonal, then turn each cover right side out.

Variations

Any color can be used for the pillow covers, and you can quilt them in either a matching or a contrasting color. Because these are square designs, they can be adapted to other projects that make use of squares – for example, the bag on page 116 or the quilt on page 124. You could work the same designs in different colors or work these two designs and several other quilting blocks all in the same colorway. The central knot of pattern B can also easily be adapted for corded quilting (see page 132).

Try adapting the true lovers' knot design to a square quilt; enlarge the central medallion, then make a border of the feather designs radiating from the corners. Fill in the background with the diamond filling texture.

You can put a texture behind the rosette design, too; in this example small rosettes taken from the center of the main medallion have been placed in each corner of a square quilt, and the diamonds stitched in between. The edge is finished with a ruffle.

By working the design in blocks, you can construct a quilt of any size. Here the rosette medallion has been worked on six blocks, then made up into a quilt with lattice strips between the blocks. The entwined border has been used all around the edges of the quilt, changing the direction of the twists in the center of each side.

You can use the central medallion from either pillow design to decorate a circular pillow, finishing off the edge either with cording or with a gathered ruffle in the same fabric.

*I*NSPIRATION

Although the traditional quilting method is a very old one, it is still a favorite with contemporary quilters. The examples shown here – old and new – demonstrate its versatility.

▼ *Here, quilting has been combined with appliqué. The appliqué tulips are arranged on the background in a diamond pattern which is echoed by the quilted lines. Each corner also contains a quilted tulip shape.*

▲ *This beautiful modern quilt is stitched in white-on-white silk and makes use of an unusual arched pattern to link the leaf designs in the border.*

▼ *This quilt shows a typical Amish design and color scheme, enhanced by careful hand-quilting in orange and purple thread.*

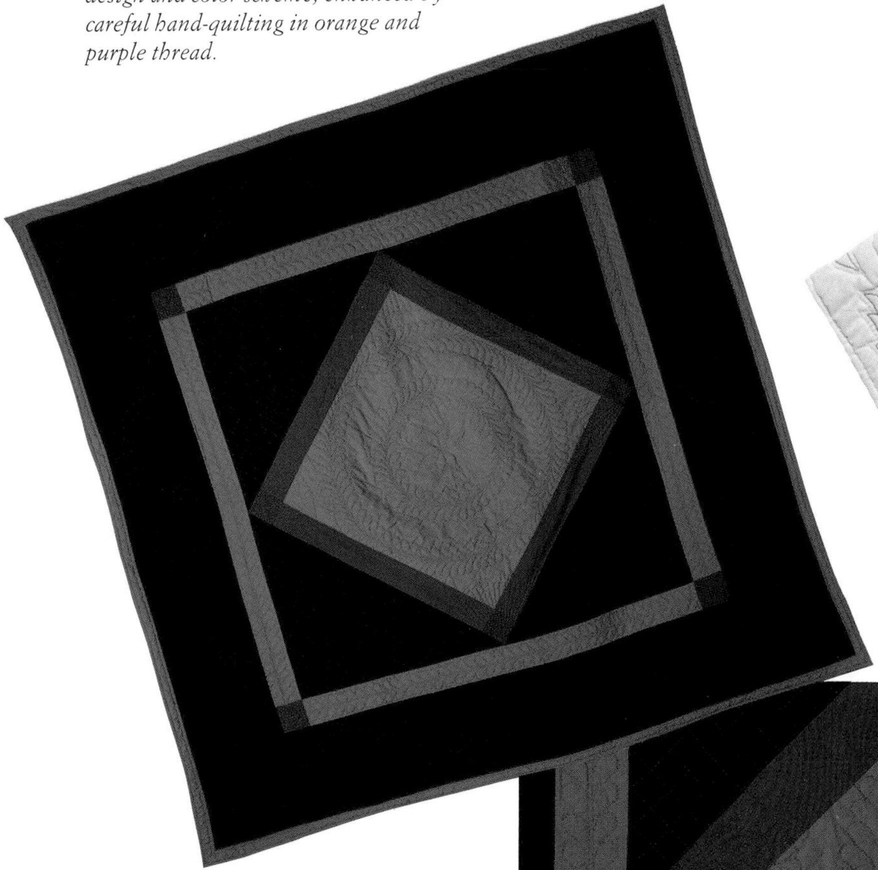

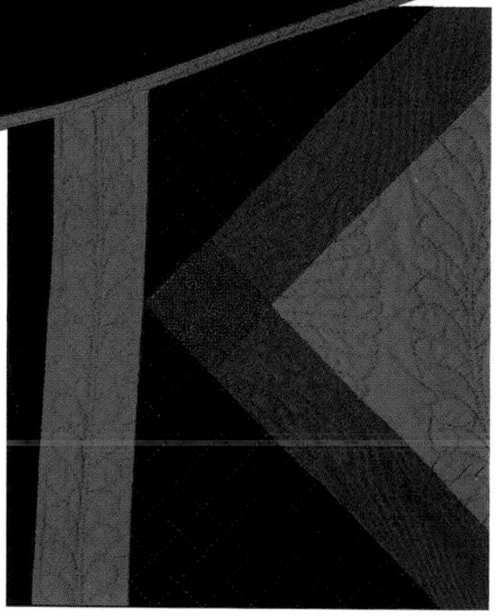

The swallow jacket shown here looks as though it was stitched after many years' experience; in fact it was the designer's first attempt at quilting. The big swallow shape was enlarged freehand from a picture, while the smaller ones were traced. The leaves for the borders were copied from the designer's tea set.

The quilted item on the left is a 19th-century Persian bath mat. The quilting is worked in backstitch through cotton batting, and the motifs and central medallion are embroidered in various colored silks.

CHAPTER 3

SHADOW QUILTING

Shadow quilting – like most other types of quilting – uses three layers of material; but this technique doesn't use batting. Instead, the patterns are produced by stitching pieces of contrasting fabric between two other fabric layers, the top layer being sheer or translucent so that muted versions of the colors beneath show through. The shapes of the pattern are emphasized by the lines of stitching around the inserted pieces of fabric, and if the fabric pieces are quite thick – felt, for example – the stitching produces an interesting texture, too. If you use sheer fabrics for the top *and* bottom layers, you can produce beautiful translucent curtains that will show off your designs as the light shines through.

+ + +   **SHADOW QUILTING · PROJECT 1**   + + +

GREETINGS CARDS

Hand-stitched cards are perfect for special occasions such as birthdays, anniversaries, weddings, or the arrival of a new baby.

The two designs described here are versatile, and they can be produced using scraps of fabric from your sewing chest. Use a very sheer fabric for the top layer – such as a very fine organdy, organza, or firm chiffon – to allow the colors underneath to show through as much as possible.

Greeting cards blanks are available in many different sizes, colors, and shapes, so choose a card that goes with the fabric scraps you have, or buy a white one and paint it yourself.

Preparation for making the glitter card
Press all the pieces of fabric that you are going to use.

MATERIALS	
For the glitter card	*For the candle card*
1 cream marbled greeting card blank	1 blue greeting card blank
1 piece of gold glitter fabric the same size as the folded card	Scraps of felt in royal blue, pink, yellow, orange, and red
1 piece of sheer fabric the same size as the folded card	Sewing threads in the same colors
Scraps of metallic fabric in pink, turquoise, and royal blue	1 piece of white fabric the same size as the folded card
Metallic threads to match the fabrics	1 piece of sheer white fabric the same size as the folded card
White all-purpose glue	White all-purpose glue
Transfer fusing web *or* glue stick	Transfer fusing web *or* glue stick

If you are using transfer fusing web, iron a small section 1 in (2.5 cm) square onto the back of the pink, blue, and turquoise glitter fabrics. Cut small triangles out of each of these fabrics, two of each color (if using bonding web, cut the triangles where it has been attached).

If you are using fusing web, peel off the backing paper, position the triangles where you want them, and iron them to secure them to the gold background fabric. If you are not using fusing web, glue the triangles in place with the glue stick.

Quilting

1 Place the sheer fabric over the gold background fabric, and baste it firmly in place so that it won't move around during the stitching.

2 Stitch around the edges of the triangles with matching metallic thread, using backstitch and leaving a small margin between the edge of the triangle and the stitching line.

Finishing

3 When you have completed the stitching, remove the basting threads and press the design on the back, making sure that the iron is not too hot.

4 Spread a little glue over the inside of the fold-down flap on the card and a little bit around the inside of the window section (don't use too much glue on the window frame or the card may buckle).

5 Position the quilted fabric carefully face down on the glued window section so that the design shows through the window. Spread the fabric as flat as possible.

6 Fold the glued flap over the back of the design, and weight the card with a heavy book until it is dry.

Preparation *The triangles are cut from the glitter fabric and glued in place on the gold background fabric with transfer fusing web or glue stick.*

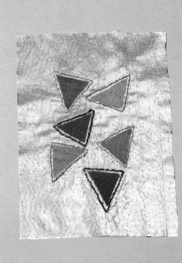

Quilting *The sheer fabric is laid over the top of the triangles, and the layers are basted together to prevent them from slipping.*

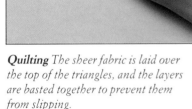

The triangles are stitched down with glitter thread and the basting threads removed.

Finishing *The fabric is positioned to make sure that the design fits inside the*

window. Glue is spread over the insides of the window section and fold-down

flap of the card blank, then the design is positioned and the flap folded.

Preparation for making the candle card

Press the fabrics you plan to use.

Trace all the shapes shown in the pattern (right) onto thin paper, and cut them out for use as templates. Choose a different number instead of "1" if appropriate.

If you are using fusing web, use the paper templates as guides for cutting out pieces. Iron these onto the felt scraps of the appropriate colors, and cut out the shapes. If you are not using fusing web, use the paper templates as guides for cutting out the felt shapes.

If you are using fusing web, peel off the backing papers, position the felt shapes on the white background fabric, and iron them on to secure them in position. If you are not using the fusing web, glue the felt pieces in place with dabs of glue stick.

Quilting

1 Baste firmly around the edges of the fabrics so that the felt shapes will not move; where there is more than one layer, work a line of basting stitches across the design as well.

2 Using matching threads, hand-stitch around the edge of each felt shape, beginning with the number and the center of the flame and working outward. Use backstitch to produce a solid-colored line.

3 When the stitching is complete, remove the basting threads and press the design on the back.

Finishing

Finish the card in the same way as the glitter card.

Variations

The glitter card design can be very easily adapted to card blanks of other shapes. Simply cut your background fabric and sheer fabric to fit, then arrange the glitter triangles in a pleasing pattern. Or choose bright felts or satins instead of glitter fabrics.

The candle card can be varied by choosing different colors for the candle and the number and by altering the number to suit different birthdays or anniversaries. The shape is less adaptable than that of the glitter card, but can be fitted into a card with an oval window as well as a rectangular one. If you want to make a card for an eighteenth or twenty-first birthday or a twenty-fifth wedding anniversary, for example, you could use a square format and stitch two candles, with one numeral on each.

Shapes for the candle card

Use these patterns for a single or composite (e.g. 25) number on the candle card.

SHADOW QUILTING · PROJECT 2

WATER LILY CURTAIN

Brighten up a dull view with a translucent curtain worked in shadow quilting. The subtle colors of the water lilies are ideal for this delicate design.

Choose lightweight fabrics for the colored shapes – light satins, cottons, chiffons, for example – so that they don't distort the background fabric. For the curtain itself, choose a semi-sheer fabric such as muslin or a closely woven organdy.

Preparation

Wash and press all the fabrics.

Cut the white fabric pieces to the depth of your window and keep the remaining strips for the ruffle.

Trace the water lily pattern pieces onto thin paper and cut them out. Use these to cut four of each pattern piece out of the fusing web.

Iron the fusing web pieces onto the backs of the colored fabrics as appropriate, and cut out around the shapes. Use the pale cream and pale pink fabrics for the main petals and the darker cream and pink for the top petals. Cut two large and two small leaves from each shade of green.

Lay one of the pieces of white fabric right side down on a flat surface. Peel away the backing paper from the fusing

Preparation *The fusing web-backed pattern pieces are positioned on the background fabric to form a pleasing design, then ironed to fuse them in position.*

Quilting *The front piece of fabric is placed over the fused design and basted in place.*

Pattern for water lily shapes.

TIPS FOR PROFESSIONAL RESULTS

● If the fabric you have chosen for the curtain front and back loses its shape easily, such as loosely woven muslin, you can make it firmer by fusing the two layers together with ordinary fusing web across the whole area of the curtain before stitching, or you can spray the finished quilted curtain with firm starch.

● Tie the threads off with a small firm knot, and cut the trailing ends close to the knot so that they don't show when the light shines through the curtain.

● Choose pastel or medium shades for the colored fabrics; darker shades will show merely as silhouettes, rather than as colors, when the curtain is hanging up.

Quilting *Each colored section of the design is stitched around by machine or* *hand using matching thread.*

Here the water lily design has been used on a traditional-style café curtain. Put the right sides of the fabric together, and stitch the shaped seam at the top first of all, then clip the seams

and turn the white fabrics right side out. Position the colored motifs between the two layers, and stitch them in place.

On this small roller shade, suitable for a bathroom window, only one flower motif has been used, with several extra leaves added to fill the design out to fit the width of the window.

web, and position the petal and leaf shapes in a pleasing arrangement. When you are happy with the design, iron firmly across the shapes to bond them to the background fabric.

Cut ¾ in (2 cm) wide strips of fusing web, iron them to the back of the ribbons, and attach them to the lower edge of the white fabric in the same way.

Quilting

1 Place the other piece of white fabric, right side up, on top of the bonded pieces. Baste the layers firmly together with lines of basting stitches across the width of the curtain.

2 If you are quilting by machine, use straight stitch and matching thread to stitch around the edges of each colored shape; tie the threads firmly on the wrong side of the curtain.

If you are quilting by hand, use backstitch and matching thread to sew around the edges of each colored shape; tie the threads firmly on the wrong side of the curtain.

3 When all the quilting is complete, remove the basting threads.

Finishing

4 If you have selvages at the edges of your curtain, baste the top and bottom layers together and stitch together by machine.

If you have raw edges, either bind them with straight strips of your white fabric or turn them under and machine stitch a tiny seam.

5 Press ¾ in (2 cm) to the wrong side along the top of the curtain, then press this under again to form a hem of about 2 in (5 cm). Machine stitch along the inner folded edge to make a casing through which the curtain rod can be threaded.

6 Use some of the remaining white fabric to make a ruffle – single, double, or folded (see page 18). Hold the curtain up to the window and measure it to see how deep the ruffle needs to be.

Variations

Instead of making a simple drop curtain like the one here, you can vary the design to make a café-style curtain; either add loops to the heading of the full-length curtain or make a classic half height café curtain.

The number and positioning of the water lily shapes can be adapted to suit windows of any size: a small translucent curtain for a bathroom window might only need one or two complete motifs; full-length curtains across a French window would benefit from more.

If the curtain is made in very fine fabric, it could be stiffened and used as a roller shade (department stores sell kits for making these yourself).

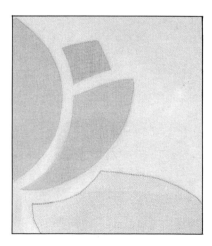

INSPIRATION

Virtually any sheer fabric can be used for shadow quilting; although white is traditional, pastels and medium shades can produce unusual effects as they alter the colors of the materials underneath them. The examples on these pages demonstrate many different approaches to the basic shadow quilting technique.

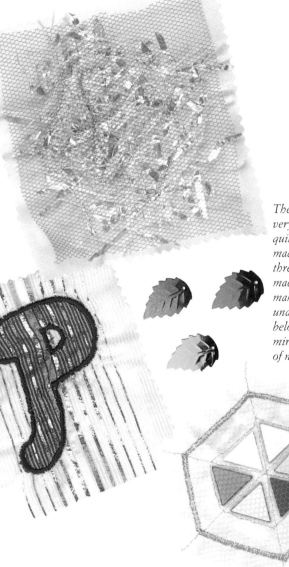

The samples on this page show several very different approaches to shadow quilting. The two shapes above were made from twists of bright and sparkly thread, caught down behind net by machine stitching. The letter on the left makes use of a colored satin shape under metallic fabric, and the hexagon below is formed from bright-colored mirror shapes caught in stitched pockets of net.

A stencil effect has been used for the fruit bowl on the right. The shapes for the bowl and the different fruits were cut from colored fabrics and fused to the background with transfer fusing web. The top was then covered in muslin to soften the colors, and each shape was stitched around in sewing thread in a matching shade. The irregular edge was bound with fine white bias binding.

Left, several layers of fabric were sandwiched together with lines of machine satin stitch, then the layers were trimmed back to different levels. Where the top layer of muslin remains, it gives a muted shade of the green fabric underneath.

Printed fabrics can lend themselves well to shadow quilting, as this bird sample shows.

◄ The shadow quilted heart also makes use of the trapunto technique. Because it would be difficult to keep the star sequins in position during stitching, the heart-shaped pocket was stitched first, by machine, then the back of the pocket was slit, stuffed with sequins, and stitched closed.

▲ This unusual textile piece uses rings of rice captured in pockets of shaded muslin to produce a beaded effect; the designer was interested in using natural materials and experimented with lentils and other pulses as well as rice.

The piece of shadow quilting below was stitched using rectangles of satin in rainbow colors under several layers of surgical gauze, which were spread at random across the shape and then stitched over the strip and trimmed. The gauze was then manipulated by stretching and pulling the threads to reveal the colors underneath.

Bright fabric scraps can be caught down behind veiling or net for an unusual and contemporary interpretation of shadow quilting.

CHAPTER 4

RANDOM QUILTING

As its name suggests, random quilting doesn't follow a set pattern – you simply quilt in random lines or shapes across the item that you're working on. Random quilting is thus very easy to do and can be worked by hand or by machine, yet it can result in some very sophisticated effects, as the projects in this chapter show.

The technique can be used on all kinds of different fabrics and to different scales – from very small items to very large ones. You can work the stitches in the same color as the background fabric – so that the texture becomes the main feature – or you can use a contrasting or glittery thread so that the lines of stitching become decorative features in their own right.

+ + + **RANDOM QUILTING · PROJECT 1** + + +

MIRROR FRAME

The use of couching (the technique of catching down a thick thread with stitches in a thinner one) allows you to use multicolored glitter yarn for this project. The colored Lurex threads in the glitter yarn catch the light in a very attractive way. If you can't get a fine glitter yarn in the color you want, you can always use a thicker one –

even very slubby ones will work well, since you don't have to stitch them through the fabric.

Preparation

Iron the pieces of blue satin and the muslin.

Measure 3 in (7 cm) in from each side of the piece of board, and draw an inner rectangle. Cut it out using the craft knife, leaving a frame of board.

Lay the board frame on the right side of one of the pieces of satin, leaving the 2 in (5 cm) margin all the way around. Draw around the edge of the frame – inside and outside – with a water-soluble pen, to create a frame shape/

MATERIALS

1 mirror tile or piece of mirrored glass	thread
2 pieces of blue satin fabric, each 2 in (5 cm) larger all around than the mirror	Sewing thread to match the satin
	1 piece of strong mounting board, the same size as the mirror
1 piece of muslin the same size as the satin	Invisible transparent tape
1 piece of thick polyester batting the same size as the satin	Strong craft glue
	Craft knife
1 spool of blue glitter yarn	Water-soluble pen
1 spool of Madeira gold machine thread *or* gold Gütermann sewing	Gold cord sufficient to finish the mirror (optional)

outline on the fabric.

Mark random wavy lines across the fabric with the water-soluble pen; these will be your stitching guides. Don't worry about spacing them evenly, as random quilting of this kind looks best when there is a good variation in the distances between lines.

Quilting

1 Lay the piece of muslin on a flat surface, place the batting on top, then put the marked satin, right side up, on top of the batting. Baste all three layers together outside the marked lines (in case the basting leaves any marks on the satin).

2 If you are quilting by machine, thread the needle and bobbin with the Madeira gold thread, and set the machine to a narrow zigzag stitch (about $1/16$ in [2 mm] wide and $1/16$ in [2 mm] long). Place a length of glitter yarn along each marked line, and couch it down onto the satin with zigzag stitching, extending the stitching about $3/8$ in (1 cm) over the edges of the marked borders.

If you are quilting by hand, use the Gütermann gold thread to couch the lengths of glitter yarn down onto the satin along the marked lines, using single stitches at short intervals. Extend the stitching about $3/8$ in (1 cm) over the edges of the marked borders.

3 When the couching is complete, remove the basting threads and trim the fabric to within 1 in (2.5 cm) all around the border, inside and outside. Using a damp cloth, gently wipe away any pen lines that are still visible.

Finishing

4 Place the quilted border face down on a flat surface, and position the board frame on top, leaving even margins of fabric all around it.

Preparation *The frame shape is traced onto the front of the fabric, then wiggly lines are drawn across it at random intervals.*

Quilting *The lines are quilted with couched lengths of glitter yarn; then the fabric is trimmed on the outside and inside edges of the frame shape.*

Finishing *The board frame is laid on the back of the quilted frame, and the raw edges of the fabric are folded over the edges and secured with tape.*

The mirror is laid on the wrong side of the backing fabric, and the raw edges of the fabric are folded over and secured to the right side of the mirror with tape.

5 Fold the raw edges of the fabric over the frame, and secure them with short pieces of tape, folding the corners around neatly.

6 Place the other piece of satin right side down on a flat surface, and put the mirror on it, right side up, leaving an even margin all the way around.

7 Fold the raw edges of the fabric over the edges of the mirror, and secure them neatly with short pieces of tape.

8 Spread a generous amount of glue over the back of the frame, and place it on the mirror, making sure you match the edges of the two shapes. Leave it to dry thoroughly, weighting the frame slightly so that the surfaces are pressed together.

9 Use the matching blue thread to neatly slipstitch the two layers of fabric together around the outsides of the frame.

10 If you wish, use craft glue to glue a border of gold cord around the inside and/or outside of the frame.

Variations

The same technique can be used for mirrors of all sizes and shapes, including oval and circular ones and mirrors in fancy shapes, such as hearts. Make sure that you cut an even border shape in board by tracing around the mirror shape and measuring in evenly from all sides. Instead of blue satin, you can choose fabric – solid or printed – that matches your room or upholstery. Also, you could work the frame in contour quilting (see page 22) instead of random quilting. Random quilting can be worked in many shapes other than wavy lines. Try working straight lines at random intervals or in different directions, for example, or stitch one long wavy line outward in a spiral pattern.

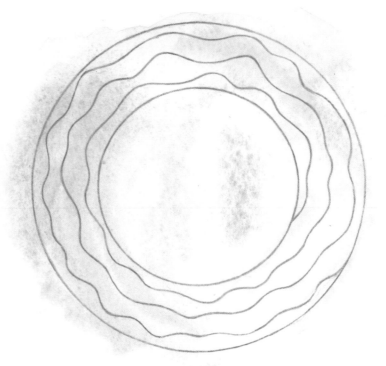

One long wavy line is stitched in a random spiral around a circular frame – beginning in the center and working outward to the edge.

TIPS FOR PROFESSIONAL RESULTS

- Don't be tempted to cut out the central panel of the satin *before* you have worked the quilting; keeping the center in helps to prevent the fabric from distorting during stitching.

- Working the couching a short way over the drawn borders helps to make sure that the ends of the threads are safely hidden behind the frame when it is mounted, as they are then taken to the back of the board as you turn the fabric over and tape it down.

- If you are new to random quilting, you'll find it helpful to try couching on some spare fabric and batting so that you're happy with the technique before you start quilting the frame itself.

- The muslin is used so that the batting is firmly sandwiched between two layers of fabric and so doesn't catch on things while you are stitching.

- If you prefer to stitch your mirror frame by hand, couch down the glitter yarn with a series of short stitches worked in plain gold thread: you can space them either evenly, or at irregular intervals to emphasize the random nature of the design.

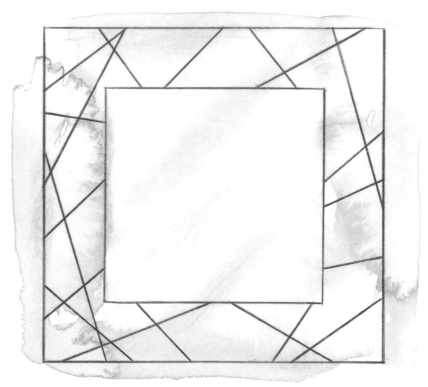

For this design, a square mirror frame is stitched across at random intervals with straight lines of quilting worked at different angles. A pattern like this produces unusual effects when the lines cross each other.

RANDOM QUILTING · PROJECT 2
CLUTCH PURSE

This sparkling evening bag makes use of the technique of reverse appliqué. Several layers of fabric are stitched together, then the layers are cut back to reveal different colors. The technique gives the layers a slightly three-dimensional effect, which is then enhanced with lines of random machine quilting. This project is best stitched by machine, as the appliqué fabrics need to be securely fastened to the background to insure that they will not fray.

When assembled, the bag is finished with a handle made from tubing cut out of one of the appliqué fabrics.

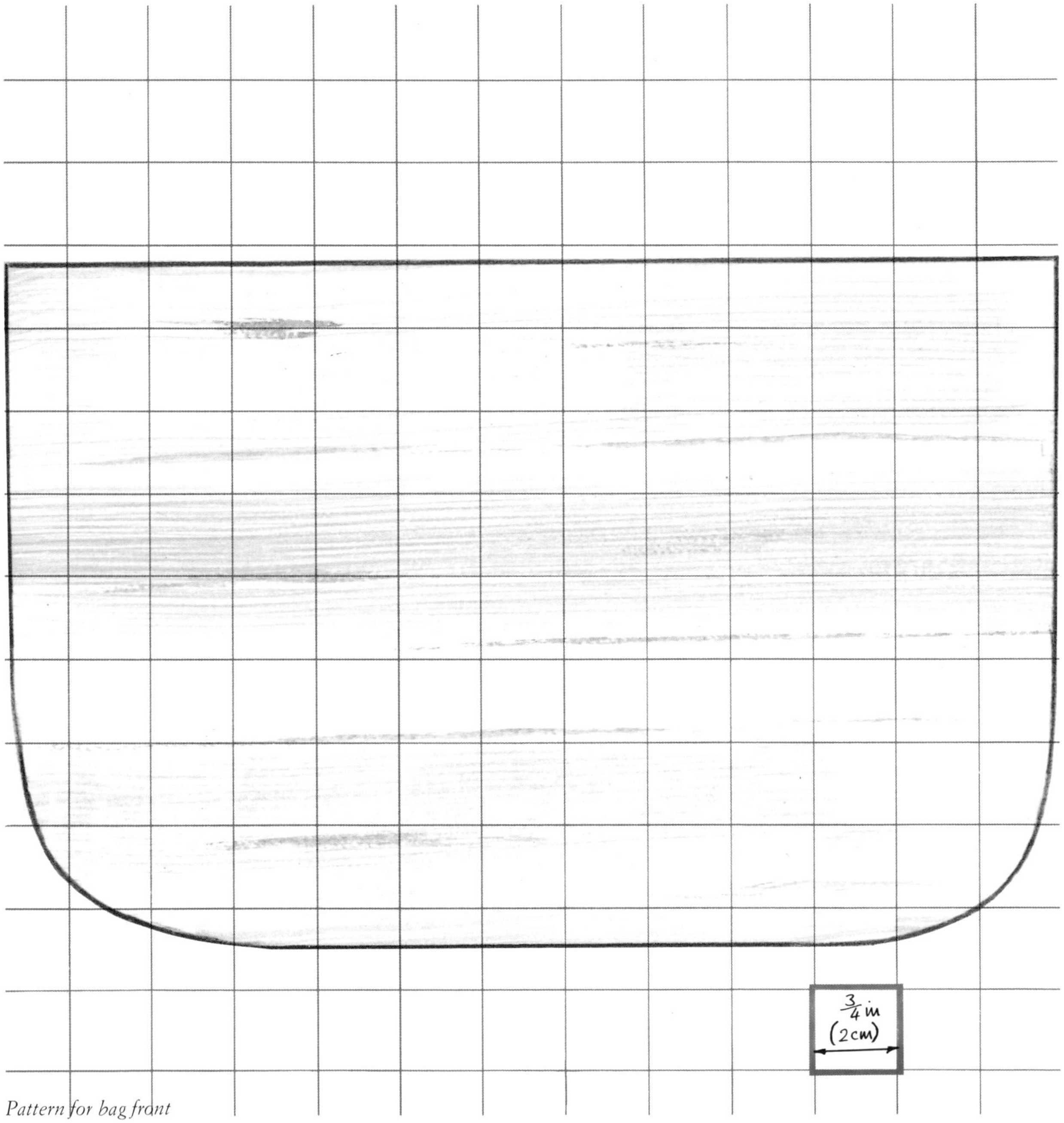

Preparation

Enlarge the pattern for the bag (see page 26), and cut the shape for the back and flap from all three fabrics, the batting, the lining, the iron-on stiffener, and the Stitch-n-Tear.

Cut the bag front from the remaining background fabric, the remaining lining, and the batting. Mark the lines of the appliqué pattern on the right side of

$\frac{3}{4}$ in
(2cm)

Pattern for bag front

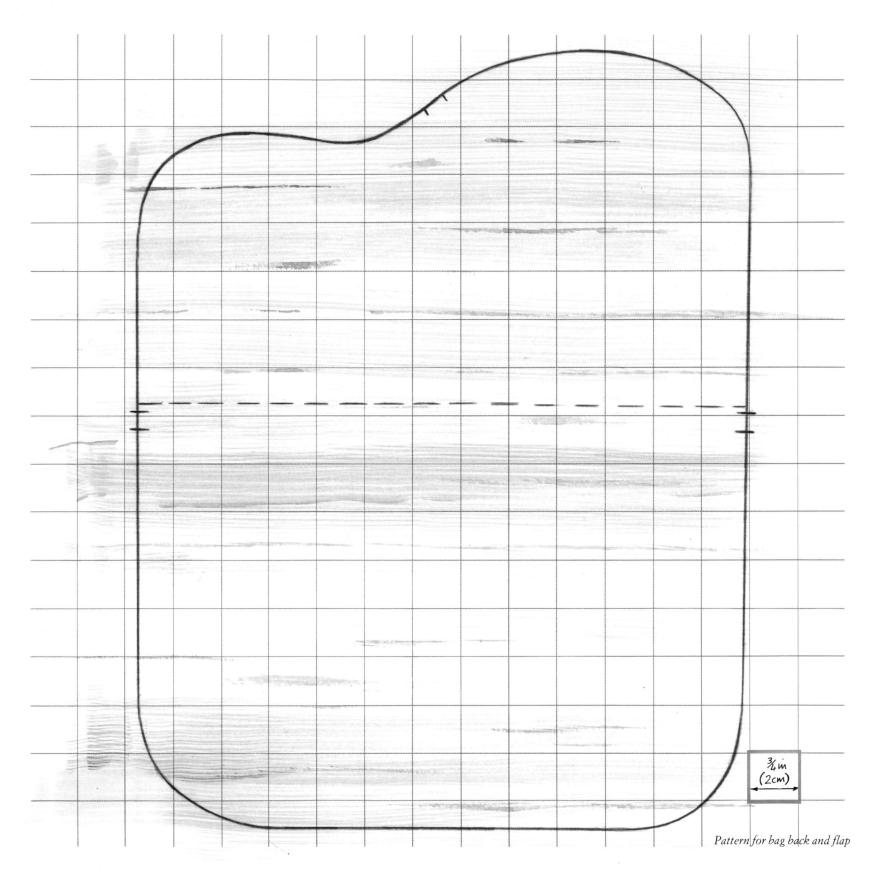

Pattern for bag back and flap

¾in
(2cm)

MATERIALS

1 piece of background fabric 24 x 12 in (60 x 30 cm)

2 pieces of similar fabric in harmonizing colors, each 16 x 12 in (40 x 30 cm)

1 piece of lining fabric the same size as the background fabric

1 piece of extra-firm iron-on stiffener the same size as the background fabric

1 piece of Stitch-n-Tear the same size as the harmonizing fabrics

1 piece of thick polyester batting the same size as the background fabric

Sewing thread in harmonizing colors: 1 spool of decorative thread for the appliqué; 1 spool of thread to match the background fabric

Bias binding strips 1 in (2.5 cm) wide and a total of 6 ft (2 m) long, made from the surplus of one of the appliqué fabrics

Small button mold for covering

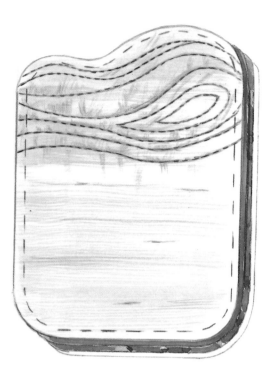
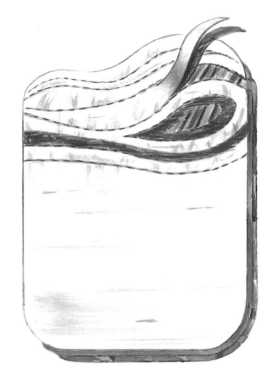

Preparation The fabric layers for the bag back and flap are stitched together around the outside, then lines of straight stitching are worked in random patterns across the flap.

Fabric layers are cut back between the lines of stitching to reveal the different-colored shapes underneath.

TIPS FOR PROFESSIONAL RESULTS

• Don't make the appliqué shapes too complicated; the best results come from bold, simple lines.

• Using an iron-on stiffener on the main part of the bag prevents it from sagging with use.

• If you want to hide all your stitching when binding the edges, stitch the first edge of the bias strips by machine, then finish the other side neatly by hand with slipstitching.

the background fabric flap, preferably with a fading pen.

Lay the piece of Stitch-n-Tear on a flat surface. Place the other two layers of fabric one on top of the other, right sides up, and position the background fabric over the top. Baste all four layers together.

Using straight stitching on your machine, stitch around the outlines of the appliqué pattern.

Carefully cut through one or more layers of fabric close to the machine stitching, to reveal the different colors. Pull off the Stitch-n-Tear.

Quilting

1 Mark the foldline of the flap on the iron-on stiffener, and work a line of machine straight stitching along it (this will insure that the flap folds easily).

2 Place the stiffener on a flat surface,

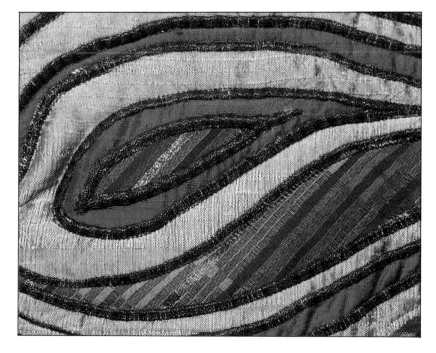

TIPS FOR MAKING AND USING TUBING

• Fold the raw edges in to the wrong side along each side of the bias strip, and fold it in half so that the folded edges are aligned, then machine or hand stitch close to the folded edges.

• To make a button loop, cut a piece of the tubing strip long enough to slip easily (not too loosely or too tightly) over the button plus the depth of the ends to be turned under.

• To attach a button loop and bias binding together, lay the binding along the edge of the quilting, right sides together and raw edges aligned. Slip the measured loop between the quilting and binding, bending it to form a U shape. Align the raw edges of the tubing strip with the raw edges of the quilting. Baste and sew in place in the normal way to attach the binding, but sewing back and forth over the button loop ends to insure that they stay secure during use.

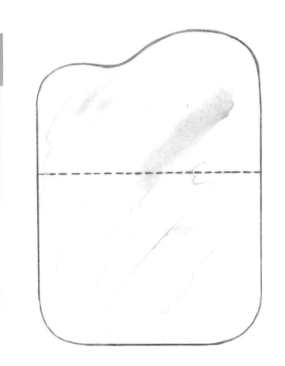

Quilting The extra-firm stiffener is stitched along the foldline to make it easier to fold the flap over when the bag is quilted.

When the appliquéd piece, batting, and backing fabric have been basted together, the edges of the cut layers are

sewn around with bands of machine stitching in decorative thread.

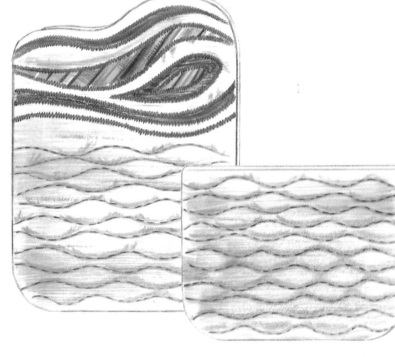

The front section of the bag is basted to its batting and backing fabric, then the back and front sections are quilted with

random lines of machine stitching in harmonizing thread.

and cover it with the matching piece of batting. Position the appliquéd fabric, right side up, on top, and baste the layers together.

3 Set the sewing machine to satin stitch or a close zigzag, using the widest stitch setting, and thread it with the decorative thread. Stitch along the appliqué outlines.

4 Baste together the front pieces of batting and background fabric.

5 Working straight machine stitching in the harmonizing thread, quilt random lines across both pieces of the bag, working across the bag shape from side to side.

Finishing

6 Baste the quilted shapes to the linings, and trim any untidy edges.

7 Bind the straight top edge of the front section with some of the bias strip (see page 17).

8 Position the bag front so that it matches up with the lower edges of the bag, lining sides together, and baste right at the edge of the bag shape. Machine stitch the two pieces together.

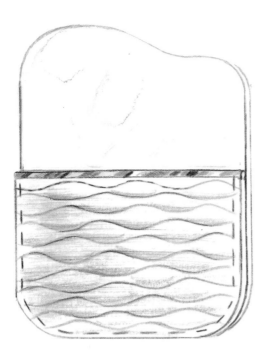

Finishing *The linings are attached to the front and back sections, and the straight top edge of the bag front is bound with one of the appliqué fabrics.*

The front and back are then stitched together right at the edges, lining sides together.

The long tubing handle and short tubing loop fastening are caught in as the edge of the bag shape is bound with a bias strip of fabric.

9 Make a small length of bias tubing (see page 62) from the remaining bias binding for a loop fastening and a longer one for the handle.

10 Bind right around the bag, inserting the handle ends at the edges where the flap folds, and the smaller loop at the center bottom of the flap (see page 62).

11 Cover the button with one of the appliqué fabrics and sew it in place on the bag front.

Variations

Many different fabrics can be used for this bag pattern, but you will get the best results if you choose three fabrics of a similar weight and fiber content.

You can make the bag without a handle if you wish, or you could make a more complex handle by making tubing strips from all three fabrics and braiding them together. A longer version of this kind of handle could be used to convert it into a shoulder bag. If you make yourself a special evening dress or skirt, you could use bits of leftover fabric to make a bag that matches it perfectly.

DESIGN VARIATIONS

Random quilting gains its effect from smoothly flowing lines; the exact arrangement they are in doesn't matter too much – what's important is that the lines be consistent in style. You can even do random quilting with angled lines, but again you need an overall consistency in the lines you use within one project. Experiment with some of the alternative patterns shown here – they can be used for numerous projects, from belts and bags to whole quilts.

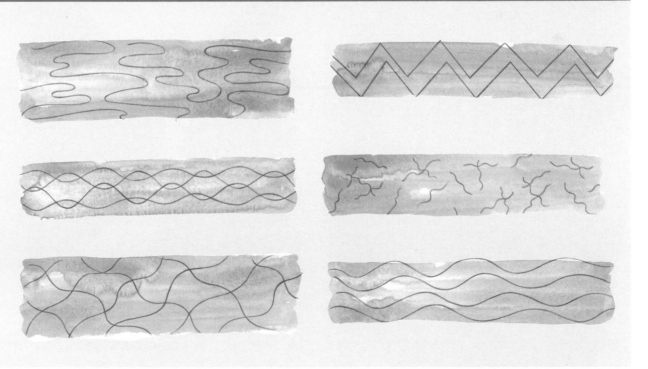

$\mathcal{I}$NSPIRATION

R andom quilting is ideal for experimentation, because the pattern created is entirely up to you. The pieces on these pages show the work of several quilters using random quilting in quite different ways.

This jerkin has been stitched so that it is reversible; all the seams are hidden and the random quilting lines look equally neat on both sides of the garment. Using this technique, you get two jerkins for the same amount of time and effort as it takes to produce one.

The so-called vermicelli or meander pattern involves quilting an item by stitching very small wiggly lines in random patterns all over it. For the best

effect none of the lines should cross. This bag has been quilted with vermicelli stitch; the areas left plain form a secondary flower pattern.

The fabric used for this sumptuous evening jacket is gold-brown silk douppioni, quilted over batting. The jacket is covered with an asymmetric design of flowing leaves thrown into relief by the vermicelli quilting around them. The edges of the leaves have also been stitched with a very fine line of metallic thread.

▶ These quilted make-up bags were stitched as experiments in random quilting. The shapes were padded with thin batting, then quilted with random lines of chain stitch in rainbow colors.
On the larger bag, random lines of white running stitch were added across the rest of the bag.

The panel above, Palm Branch, combines the stained glass appliqué technique with random machine quilting. The green fabrics were basted into position on a padded background, then the leaf fronds were stitched in different directions before the lines of bias binding were added.

CHAPTER 5

TIED QUILTING

This technique gets its name from the old method of quilting by tying together several layers of fabric (you can still see a similar technique used on old mattresses).

Originally the threads were tied so that little thread showed – the purpose was practical rather than decorative – but quilters soon began to see the decorative possibilities of the technique and incorporated buttons, little circles of leather or fabric, beads, or more ornate knots into the designs. Items of furniture such as tufted sofas use the same principle.

Tied quilting is one of the most versatile of the modern quilting methods, and the projects and variations in this chapter show just some of its many possibilities.

+ + + **TIED QUILTING · PROJECT 1** + + +

*B*ABY'S JACKET

Quilted baby jackets are always fashionable and practical for chilly days. This roomy pattern will fit babies of about 6–9 months. As the baby gets bigger you can roll down the sleeves.

The pattern is simple and so it is quick to assemble.

Bias binding around the edges solves the problem of having to put seams into quilted pieces.

We chose fabric with a little strawberry print, but many other prints or solids can be quilted in the same way. Choose a lining fabric that picks up one of the colors in the print.

Preparation

Wash and press the outer and lining fabrics.

Enlarge (see page 26) the jacket pattern to the correct size onto plain paper or dressmaker's grid paper, and cut it out. Use the paper pattern to cut out the printed cotton, the solid cotton, and the batting. Cut each fabric piece ¼ in (5 mm) larger than the paper pattern, as quilting the pieces will reduce their overall size a little. Cut the batting ¾ in (2 cm) smaller all around than the fabric pieces.

With right sides together, pin, baste, and machine stitch the underarm seams of the printed fabric, taking a seam allowance of ¾ in (2 cm). Clip the seams and turn the fabric right side out.

Stitch the underarm seams of the lining fabric in the same way, but don't turn the lining right side out.

Butt the underarm edges of the batting and baste them together lightly with one or two overcasting stitches, just to hold the edges together.

MATERIALS

1 piece of printed cotton fabric 28 in (70 cm) square
1 piece of thick polyester batting the same size as the printed cotton
1 piece of solid harmonizing cotton fabric for the lining the same size as the printed cotton
Bright bias binding ¾ in (2 cm) wide and 2 yd (2 m) long
1 skein of bright pearl cotton
Sewing thread for the seams and attaching the bias binding

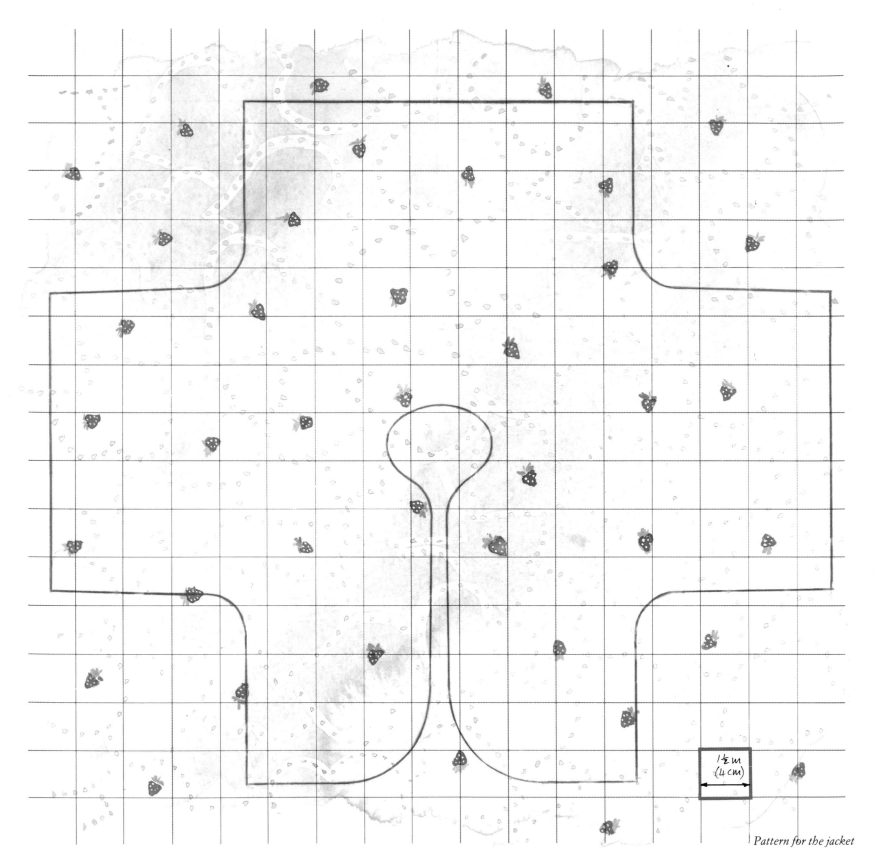

1½in
(4cm)

Pattern for the jacket

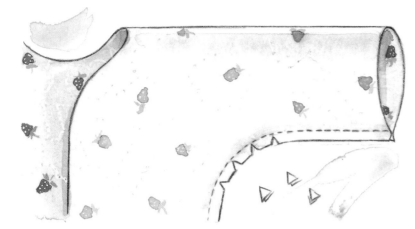

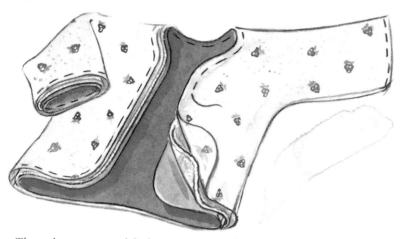

Preparation *With the right sides together, the sleeve seams of the printed fabric are stitched and clipped.*

The underarm seams of the lining are sewn and clipped, the underarm edges of the batting are lightly held together with overcasting, the batting shape is slipped inside the printed fabric shape, and the lining fabric shape is slipped inside the batting shape.

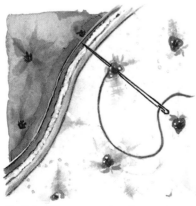

Quilting *The center of each strawberry is quilted through all layers with a French knot stitched in pearl cotton.*

Finishing *The raw edges are enclosed with contrasting bias binding.*

Quilting

1 Slip the batting inside the printed jacket shape and the lining inside the batting. The seams of the outside and the lining should now be hidden. Baste all three layers together firmly with lines of stitching at regular intervals.

2 Work French knots in the center of each strawberry or other motif by making a tiny backstitch in the lining behind the motif to secure the thread, passing the needle through to the front in the middle of the motif, but not bringing the needle all the way through. Then wind the thread around the needle several times, pull the needle through, holding the wound thread in place, and fasten the knot to the fabric by passing the needle back through to the lining side as near to where the needle originally came up as possible. Finish off the back of each knot neatly, because the stitches will show as a feature on the lining too.

Finishing

3 If necessary, trim the raw edges of the jacket shape so that they are even. Beginning at the center back of the jacket hem, attach one length of bias binding around the raw edges of the hem, fronts, and neckline (see page 17).

4 Attach bias binding around the cuffs in the same way.

5 Remove the basting threads.

Variations

If you want to make a jacket that fastens, you can incorporate button loops into the bias strip at the front (see page 62) and match them with little bright buttons on the other side. Or you could attach ribbon or tubing (see page 62) ties at the neckline.

If you prefer, use one of the other methods of tied quilting mentioned on page 73 for the jacket – although you should avoid beads or sequins for a baby jacket, to prevent the possibility of the wearer chewing them off and swallowing them!

A jacket like this made in silk or satin would be just right as a special outer garment for a christening or dedication, or if you are taking your baby to a party.

TIPS FOR PROFESSIONAL RESULTS

● When you have slipped all three layers together, pin them together all over before you baste, just to make sure that the batting is evenly distributed without any lumps and bumps.

● If you want quite a substantial French knot, use about five winds of the thread around the needle; if you want a more low-key effect, use just three or four winds.

● If you don't want the quilting stitches to show on the jacket lining, make a lining in muslin first of all, and use *that* as the inside layer while you are working the quilting. Then just slip the cotton lining inside the jacket before you attach the bias binding.

TIED QUILTING · PROJECT 2

*B*ABY'S COVERLET

Rows of pretty cream lace on a cream background, highlighted with satin bows. This baby's quilt looks really special, but is very quick to make. The lace strips are appliquéd onto a plain background by machine, then the layers are quilted by sewing on bows. You can tie them yourself from satin ribbon, or save some time and buy them ready-made. For extra speed, buy ready-gathered lace for the edging ruffle.

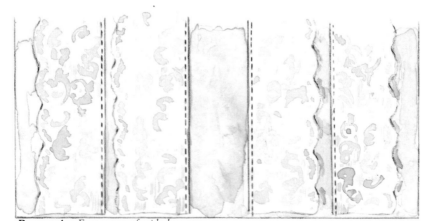

MATERIALS

2 pieces of cream cotton, polyester-cotton, satin or silk fabric 18 x 23½ in (45 x 60 cm)

2 layers of thick or extra-thick polyester batting, 16 x 22 in (40 x 55 cm)

Cream lace about 3 in (8 cm) wide and 2¾ yd (2.5 m) long, preferably with one scalloped edge

Pre-gathered cream lace about 1½ in (4 cm) wide and 2½ yd (2½ m) long

Cream satin ribbon ¾ in (2 cm) wide and 2 yd (2 m) long *or* 5 ready-made cream satin bows. Ready-made bows and ribbon rosebuds come in many styles and colors; hunt around in notions departments and in fabric shops to see what's available

Matching sewing thread

Preparation

Wash and press the cream fabric.

On the right side of one of the pieces of cream fabric, measure 3¾ in (9.5 cm) in from each long edge, and mark the lines in fading or water-soluble pen. Measure another 3¾ in (9.5 cm) in from each of the first lines and mark two more lines.

Cut four 24 in (60 cm) lengths of the wide ungathered lace, and pin the straight edges of the lengths along the marked lines on the fabric. Baste them in place, then stitch them by machine close to their edges. Remove the basting threads.

With the free edge of the lace lying toward the center of the rectangle, pin, baste and machine stitch the edge of the

Preparation *Four rows of wide lace are machine-stitched to the front fabric of the quilt at measured intervals.*

gathered lace ¾ in (2 cm) in from the edges of the quilt top on the right side, pleating the lace at the corners so that it fits well.

Place the other piece of cream fabric on top of the quilt front, right sides together. Pin, baste, and machine stitch a 1 in (2.5 cm) seam around the edge, leaving a gap of about 6 in (15 cm) along one of the short sides so that the quilt can be turned right side out.

Turn the quilt right side out, and insert the two layers of batting, pushing them to the edges and corners of the quilt so that they lie flat. Turn the edges of the gap to the inside and slip-stitch them together neatly.

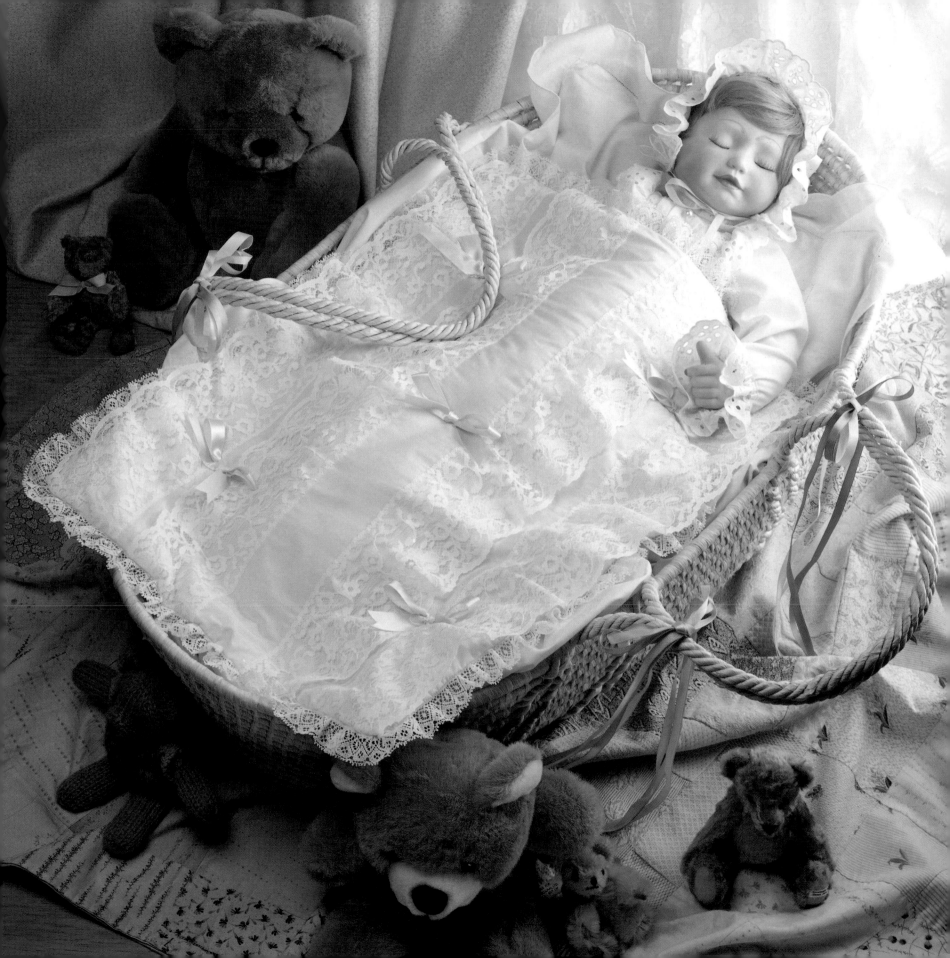

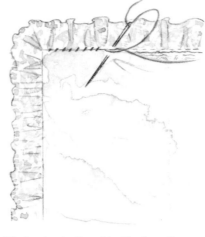

Preparation *The gathered lace is pinned, basted, and machine-stitched around the edges of the quilt front, with the free edges of the lace laid inside the edges of the fabric.*

With the right sides together, the quilt back is stitched to the quilt front around the edges, leaving a gap along one end so that the quilt can be turned right side out.

The batting is slipped inside the quilt, and the gap is slipstitched together.

TIPS FOR PROFESSIONAL RESULTS

• If you find it tricky pleating the lace at the corners of the quilt, cut each corner of the fabric to a rounded shape; then you can simply stitch the lace around the curve. Remember to trim the batting to the same shape before you insert it.

• When you're making your own bows, it can be frustrating trying to get the satin side to show on each loop and free end. You can solve this problem by tying two loops together in an overhand knot to form a bow instead of making the bow in the conventional way.

Quilting *If readymade bows are not used, satin ribbon is cut into lengths and tied into bows. The bows are then sewn in place on the quilt front, stitching through all the layers. The ends of the bows are trimmed into V-shapes.*

Quilting

1 Pin the layers of the quilt together at regular intervals so that the batting doesn't slip.

2 If you are not using ready-made bows, cut the satin ribbon into five 14 in (35 cm) lengths, and tie a small bow in each.

3 Attach each bow to the quilt top with several strong stitches, making sure that each stitch goes through all the layers of fabric to produce the quilted effect.

Finishing

4 Cut the free ends of the bows to the required length, cutting a V-shape out of them to prevent them from fraying.

Variations

The quilt can be made in shades of any color, such as pale green, yellow, blue, peach, or pink.

Another attractive idea is to appliqué cream or white lace to a pastel background or a fabric with a tiny print or to use colored ribbons on a white or cream background.

Instead of finishing the edge with pre-gathered lace, you could use eyelet lace or attach a single or double ruffle made of the background fabric (see page 18).

Readymade ribbon rosebuds, which are available in many different colors, can be used instead of the bows.

Try making a larger quilt for a crib; choose a neutral background color and pick out some of the colors from the nursery color scheme for the bows, perhaps using matching bows on curtains or crib bumpers. You could also use bows to tie-quilt a suitable purchased quilt made with printed fabric; sew the bows around the necks of teddies, or on the fronts of clown suits.

This kind of tied-quilting technique can also be used for larger quilts, although you may not want to use quite so much lace, so that it doesn't look overwhelming. Try just quilting a full-size bedspread with bows in satin ribbon in the same color; this looks very pretty in white or cream, but can also look effective with dramatic colors such as midnight blue or dark crimson.

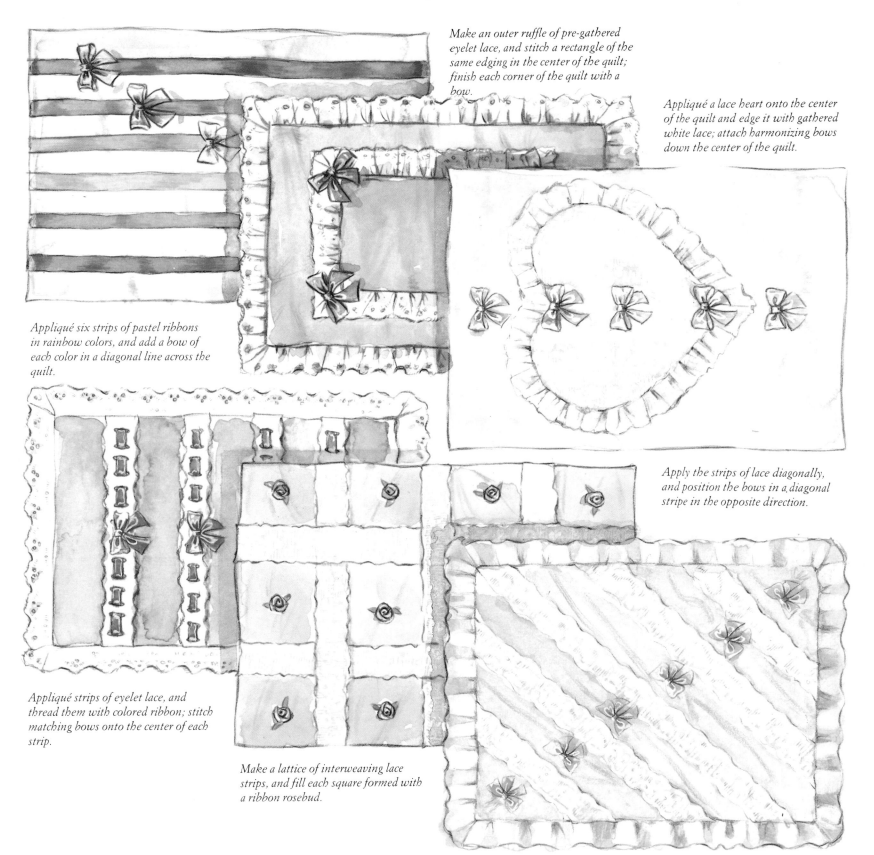

Make an outer ruffle of pre-gathered eyelet lace, and stitch a rectangle of the same edging in the center of the quilt; finish each corner of the quilt with a bow.

Appliqué a lace heart onto the center of the quilt and edge it with gathered white lace; attach harmonizing bows down the center of the quilt.

Appliqué six strips of pastel ribbons in rainbow colors, and add a bow of each color in a diagonal line across the quilt.

Apply the strips of lace diagonally, and position the bows in a diagonal stripe in the opposite direction.

Appliqué strips of eyelet lace, and thread them with colored ribbon; stitch matching bows onto the center of each strip.

Make a lattice of interweaving lace strips, and fill each square formed with a ribbon rosebud.

INSPIRATION

A lthough tied quilting is one of the oldest quilting techniques, it can be adapted very easily to produce extremely modern-looking results as you can see from the contemporary pieces on these pages.

French knots have been used singly and in clusters to quilt the pillow shown above right. The thread complements the colors of the fabric, and the knots enhance the flower design as well as providing texture.

◀ Textile Piece I *was inspired by old domestic needlecases, and uses household fabrics such as burlap and ticking, highlighted by everyday sewing items such as needles and scraps of embroidery. The stitching uses tied threads and beads as well as making use of conventional quilting. The designer intends the piece to be handled, so that the tactile quality of the quilting can be appreciated.*

Below is a detail of an outfit called Scrap Attack. *The garments were made from bright pockets of solid-colored fabrics and tufted with pieces of fine cord and eyecatching beads and buttons; the ends of the cords have been left dangling to different lengths.*

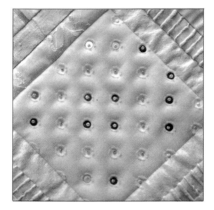

▲ *This detail shows a section of* Singapore Orchid, *a panel pieced from silk fabrics in delicate colors. The panel uses various quilting methods, including tied quilting with beads and sequins.*

The little samples scattered across these pages show some of the many items that can be used in tied quilting. Buttons and beads of all shapes and sizes lend themselves very well to tied quilting, as do ribbon roses and little bows. Varying the background fabrics opens up the technique still further; the fabrics used for these samples included gingham, metallic lamé, textured cotton, satin, silk, and soft suede.

Textile Piece II *is the reverse of* Textile Piece I, *and shows the reverse of the tied quilting techniques used. The ties echo the ribbons used to tie up the needlecases which provided the inspiration.*

CHAPTER 6

TRAPUNTO QUILTING

Trapunto is also known as padded or stuffed quilting, which gives a good clue to the method used. Each area to be quilted, or padded, is first outlined with stitching, then the backing layer is slit to allow stuffing to be pushed into the space, and the slit is then sewn up. Because of the slits made in the backing fabric, trapunto-quilted items should always be lined or used for projects such as the ones in this chapter where the raw cut edges are safely concealed by an additional layer, such as a box top or a picture frame. Because you can vary the amount of stuffing used in each area, trapunto quilting can be used to produce some highly three-dimensional effects.

+ + + **TRAPUNTO QUILTING · PROJECT 1** + + +

HEART BOX

The shape of the box itself is echoed in the heart embroidery and fabric chosen to decorate its top. The design is first worked in backstitch; then alternate hearts and background squares are stuffed to produce an intriguing texture. The pattern here fits a 16 in (40 cm) heart-shaped box kit (available from some quilting retailers), which comes complete with instructions for covering the box itself, but if your box has different proportions, re-draw the design by tracing around the box lid, dividing the shape into diamonds, then making these into heart shapes.

MATERIALS
For a 16 in (40 cm) box:
1 piece solid-colored or printed cotton or polyester-cotton fabric 18 in (45 cm) square
1 piece cotton or polyester-cotton backing fabric 18 in (45 cm)
1 yd (1 m) of wide cotton or polyester-cotton, solid or printed, to harmonize with the fabric to be quilted
Small amount of synthetic stuffing
2 skeins stranded embroidery floss in harmonizing colors
Transfer fusing web to cover both sides of each face of the box
All-purpose spray adhesive
Water-soluble pen
Thin cord or braid sufficient to cover the edges of the lid (optional)
Bodkin
Very sharp embroidery scissors

Preparation

Wash and press all the fabrics.

Enlarge (see page 26) the pattern for the box top design to the correct size. Using the water-soluble pen, trace around the box lid piece on the right side of the top fabric, adding an even margin all around it, and transfer the lines of the design onto the fabric (see page 12).

Quilting

1 Place the backing fabric on a flat surface, and position the marked fabric on top of it, right side up. Baste the two layers together, both around and across the heart shape.

2 Stitch along all the lines of the design with even backstitches, using four strands of the floss threaded through the needle together.

3 When all the stitching is complete,

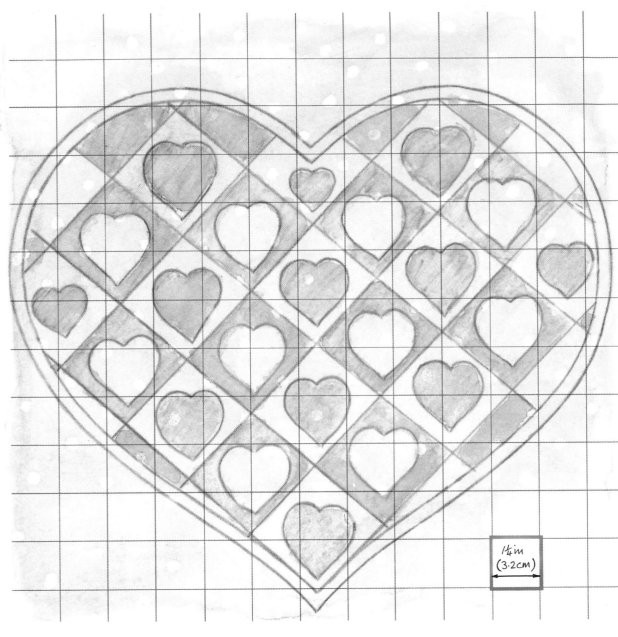

14 in
(3·2cm)

remove the basting threads, then remove any visible pen marks with a damp cloth.

4 Following the chart above, slit the backing fabric, and stuff the areas shaded on the chart, then loosely stitch the slits closed again.

Finishing

5 Using the spray adhesive, glue the backing fabric to the top of the box lid shape, leaving an even overhang all the way around. Clip the overhanging edges, and glue them to the underside.

6 Follow the instructions in the box kit for covering the rest of the box with the harmonizing fabric, ignoring the instructions for the top of the lid, of course, as yours is already covered.

7 Finish the edges of the lid with the thin cord or braid, if desired, to cover any irregularities.

Variations

This technique can be adapted for boxes of different shapes – simply

Pattern for the box lid design (the shaded areas are the parts to be stuffed)

divide your lid shape into regular diamonds and put a heart in each one. For smaller boxes, just stitch a single heart in the center and quilt around it.

Alternatively, you could use another simple motif – a star, cloud, or stylized flower, tree, or fruit, or the basic outline of an animal or bird shape.

For a personalized design, simply

Quilting The design is marked on the fabric for the lid top, and the marked layer is basted to the backing fabric.

draw a large initial on the box top – or the full name, if short – stitch around the edges, and stuff the center of the shape.

The box shown here is very dainty and has an English country cottage look. For a more contemporary look, use dramatic bold, abstract patterns and bright metallic fabrics for the box.

Quilting *The lines of the pattern are worked in backstitch, using four strands of embroidery floss in the needle, then the basting threads and pen marks are removed.*

Alternate hearts and background diamonds are stuffed from the back through slits cut in the backing fabric, and the slits are then sewn up.

Finishing *After the quilted panel and the other fabric have been glued to the box, a length of cord or braid is glued over the joint between the lid top and sides, to finish the edge neatly.*

TIPS FOR PROFESSIONAL RESULTS WITH TRAPUNTO QUILTING

- Baste the top fabric to the backing fabric.
- Outline each shape to be quilted in backstitch, close running stitch, or machine straight or satin stitch.
- Using very sharp-pointed embroidery scissors, snip very carefully into the backing fabric of each pocket formed by the stitching (taking care not to cut the front fabric), making a small slit just large enough to push some stuffing into.
- Push small amounts of stuffing into the pockets, using the head of a bodkin, until each pocket is evenly stuffed.
- Close the slits in the backing fabric with several slipstitches or with overcasting to prevent the stuffing from slipping out of place.

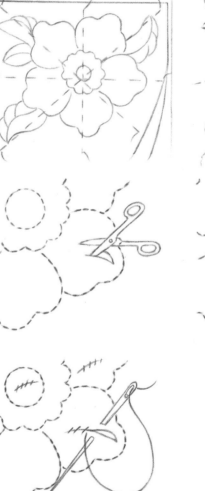

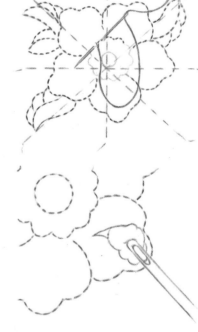

TRAPUNTO QUILTING · PROJECT 2

ROSE PICTURE

The flowers and leaves in this picture are based on the stylized roses designed in stained glass by Charles Rennie Mackintosh at the turn of the century. The flowing lines of art nouveau lend themselves well to embroidery.

This project is a combination of trapunto and shadow quilting, for the top layer of fabric is sheer so that the colors of the stuffing show through. The marbled effect is achieved by stuffing the stitched areas with "scrim" (roughly cut pieces of thread in different colors and thicknesses).

off each line of stitching carefully. Re-thread the machine with green, and stitch along the lines of the leaves, stems, and tendrils.

If you are quilting by hand, stitch along the lines of the rose in pink thread in close backstitch, and finish off the ends of each line of stitching firmly. Do the same in green along the lines of the leaves, stems, and tendrils.

3 Press the embroidery flat.

4 Using the embroidery scissors, cut a ¾ in (2 cm) long slit in the white cotton at the back of each large pocket formed by the stitching (cut shorter slits in the

TIPS FOR MAKING SCRIM

Scrim is literally a loosely-woven rough fabric, but it has lent its name to single strands of mixed fibers used for texture in decorative stitching and, in this case, for stuffing.

Make scrim by pulling threads from the edges of scraps of fabrics and cutting up skeins of embroidery threads in different thicknesses, colors, and textures.

Fabric scraps and embroidery threads used for making scrim.

Cut scrim. The threads have been mixed so that no one texture or tone dominates.

Preparation

Make two batches of scrim – one pink and one green – and mix each batch well to avoid large chunks of one color, but keep one part of each batch of scrim very light in color.

Press the fabrics.

Enlarge (see page 26) the pattern to the correct size onto paper. Lay the organdy or organza over it, and trace over the lines of the pattern using a soft pencil. (If you are quilting by hand, use water-soluble or fading pen, as the drawn lines won't be so well covered by the stitching.)

Quilting

1 Place the white cotton fabric right side up on a flat surface, and lay the marked fabric on top of it, right side up. Baste the two layers together around the circle and around the flower and leaf shapes.

2 If you are quilting by machine, thread your machine with pink thread and set it to a close, narrow zigzag or satin stitch (about ⅛ in [2 mm]), and stitch along each of the lines of the rose, finishing

MATERIALS

1 picture frame approximately 10 x 12 in (25 x 30 cm)

1 piece of white mounting board the same size as the frame

1 piece of firm white organdy *or* organza 14 x 16 in (35 x 40 cm)

1 piece of firm white cotton fabric the same size as the organdy or organza

Sewing thread in pink and green *or* if you are quilting by hand, stranded floss *or* pearl cotton

Threads in different shades of pink and green and different thicknesses for stuffing

Masking tape *or* transparent tape

Soft pencil *or* water-soluble *or* fading pen

Bodkin

Very sharp embroidery scissors

smaller areas of the rose). It is surprisingly easy to cut the sheer fabric, so be very careful.

5 Stuff the pockets of the rose with pink scrim, putting the darker scrim toward the center of the flower and the lighter scrim to the outsides of the petals. Use the eye end of the bodkin to move the threads where you want them, turning the picture over occasionally to check your work. Stuff each pocket so that it is filled but not over-stuffed – if they are over-full the picture will pucker.

6 When all the pockets in the rose are stuffed, sew the slits closed with a few overcast stitches to keep the filling in place.

7 Repeat the stuffing and stitching procedure with the leaves, using dark green scrim for the inside edges of the pockets of the leaves and lighter green for the outside edges.

Finishing

8 Lay the quilting right side down on a flat surface and place the mounting board on top. Stick the raw edges of the fabrics down onto the board with the tape, stretching the fabric evenly as much as possible to keep it taut.

9 Dismantle the frame, and lay the embroidered picture in it in place of the glass; fix the backing panel in place securely with the tape.

Variations

Choose a different color for the rose if you want to, to match the colors of a particular room, for example. It would look equally good in yellow, red, cream, or peach.

The design doesn't have to be worked as a picture. Enlarged a little, it would make a very unusual cover for a circular pillow or a circular insert in the center of a white crib quilt. Equally, you could work the pattern several times, making different-colored roses, and join them together with strips of fabric (see page 127) to make a large quilt.

Pattern for the rose picture

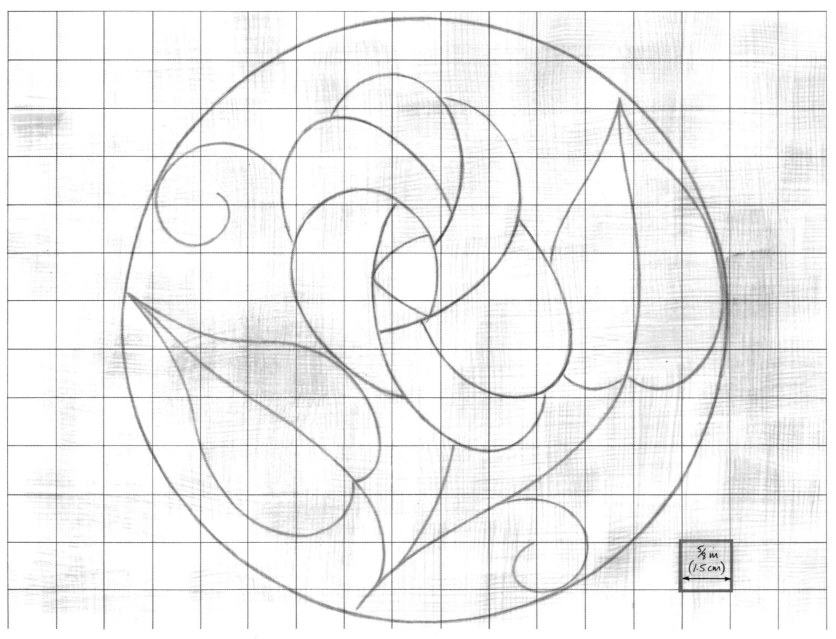

5⁄8 in (1.5 cm)

Quilting *The marked fabric is basted to the backing fabric to hold it securely in position.*

The lines of the design are stitched along by hand or machine, using pink for the rose and circle and green for the leaves and tendrils.

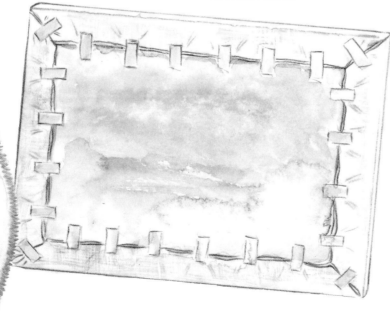

The pockets formed by the sides of each leaf are stuffed from the back with scrim.

Finishing *The quilted picture is stretched and taped over the mounting board before being placed in the picture frame.*

TIPS FOR PROFESSIONAL RESULTS

● When you are making the scrim, pull the threads from coarse fabrics to make up the bulk – this is cheaper than using only expensive embroidery threads, and very few people would notice any difference!

● Whether you are quilting by hand or by machine, you may find it useful to mount the work in an embroidery frame so that it doesn't distort while you are stitching it.

● Because organdy and organza tend to slip against other fabrics, use very small basting stitches when you are securing the two layers of fabric together to make sure that they do not move.

● Use the *head* of the bodkin to position the scrim in the pockets – the tip is too sharp, even though it is rounded, and is likely to pierce the fabric.

TRAPUNTO QUILTING · PROJECT 3

*R*AINBOW CHAIR CUSHION

Trapunto quilting looks very effective when it's combined with contour quilting on a printed fabric. The printed design acts as a stitching guide; then, when the main lines of the design have been stitched, they are stuffed from the back to make the shapes stand out. The cushion in the picture has made the most of a printed rainbow and cloud design, but you could always choose a different fabric. Whichever you choose, pick a design with strong shapes so that the quilting is easy and looks effective. Machine stitching is quicker for quilting the cushion, but it's possible to quilt it by hand if you prefer or if you want to use a more decorative stitch to outline the shapes.

MATERIALS

- 1 piece of printed fabric 16 x 28 in (40 x 70 cm) *or* 1 in (2.5 cm) larger all around than your chair back
- 1 piece of lining fabric the same size as the printed fabric
- 1 piece matching or harmonizing fabric the same size as the printed fabric, plus 3 in (8 cm) wide strips sufficient to bind the edges
- 1 piece 1 in (2.5 cm) thick foam cut to the shape of the chair back
- Matching sewing thread *or*, if you are quilting by hand, quilting *or* embroidery thread
- Polyester stuffing
- Multicolored woven tape or ribbon 48 in (120 cm) long
- Water-soluble or fading pen

Preparation

Wash and press all the fabrics.

Cut the printed fabric and lining to the shape of your chair back, but with a 1 in (2.5 cm) margin all around, or enlarge the pattern on this page and cut it out from your fabrics. Cut a piece the same size and shape from the harmonizing fabric for the back of the cushion cover.

On the right side of the printed fabric, mark a seam allowance of 1 in (2.5 cm) along each edge using the water-soluble or fading pen.

Quilting

1 Lay the lining fabric on a flat surface and the printed fabric right side up on top. Run lines of basting stitches near the main lines of the design to hold the two layers firmly together.

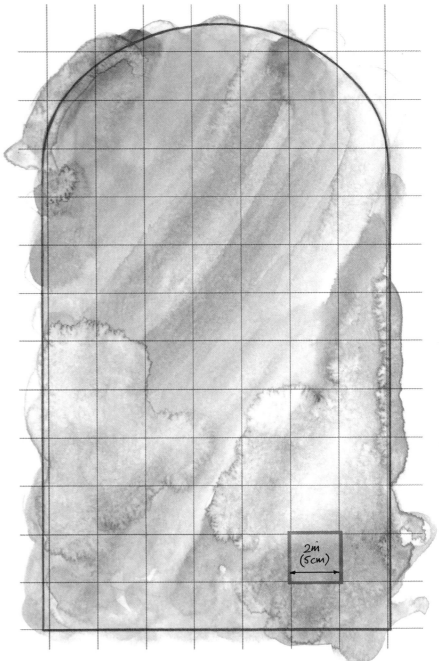

Pattern for chair cushion

2 in (5 cm)

TIPS FOR PROFESSIONAL RESULTS

● Make sure to buy fire-retardant foam for your cushion (this is available from most home decorating departments).

● Find a place that cuts foam to size, and tell them the exact shape that you want; this is easier than trying to cut the foam yourself and gives a neater result.

● If you want a thicker cushion, choose foam 1½ or 2 in (4 or 5 cm) thick, and cut your edging strips 2 in (5 cm) wider than your foam.

● You can add extra decoration to your design by using chain stitch or a fancy machine stitch for outlining the shapes, but make sure that it is a firm stitch that will produce well defined pockets.

● Couching a thick contrasting thread around the edges of the main shape can look very striking and add extra texture.

Quilting *The seam allowance is drawn in on the printed fabric, and this is basted securely to the lining fabric.*

The edge of each main shape is stitched around; where the shape crosses the seam allowance, the stitching follows the marked line so that there is still a pocket to stuff.

2 Using a straight stitch on the sewing machine or backstitch or chain stitch if you are quilting by hand, stitch around the main shapes on the printed design to form the pockets for stuffing. If one of the shapes goes off the edge of the fabric, complete the pocket by stitching along the seam line.

3 Slit the pockets (see page 79) at the back, and stuff the shapes quite firmly with the polyester stuffing. Overcast the slits to close them.

Finishing

4 Cut the strips to fit along each edge of the cushion cover, joining strips where necessary. Join the ends too, so that you have a complete ring of edging strip ready to go around the quilted fabric.

5 Placing right sides together, pin, baste and machine stitch this edging to the quilted fabric along the marked seam line. Press the seam open.

6 Placing right sides together, pin and baste the edging strip to the fabric for the back panel of the cushion cover along the sides and top of the shape, leaving the bottom edge open. Stitch a 1 in (2.5 cm) seam, and press it open.

7 Turn the cushion cover right side out, and insert the piece of foam. Turn under 1 in (2.5 cm) on the raw fabric edges and slipstitch them neatly together to close the gap.

8 Cut the tape into four equal lengths, fold each length in half, and stitch them to the four corners at the back of the cushion along the foldline.

Variations

You can easily adapt this technique to make cushions of different shapes to fit your own chairs. Make a paper pattern for the chair back first, then cut the fabric 1 in (2.5 cm) larger all around. Once you have made trapunto cushions for the backs, you can add flat seat cushions, simply made in the conven-

tional way over foam pads.

This mixture of contour quilting and trapunto is a quick way of quilting large areas effectively, and so it is very useful for other large items such as linen chest tops and floor cushions. You could make a striking cover for a child's bed by choosing a children's print and quilting it in this way; but remember the extra lining layer that you need to cover the back of the work. It's also a wonderful technique for the top of a toy box; if you use a foam pad as well as trapunto quilting, you can turn the box into an extra seat. Many of the bright prints of animals and different scenes sold for children's bedrooms are perfect for trapunto quilting.

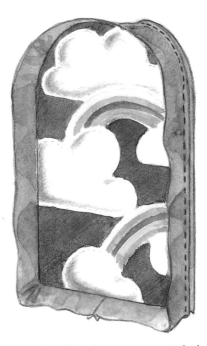

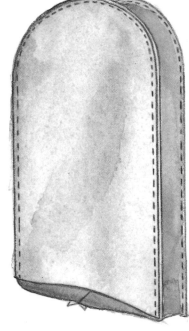

Finishing *The edging strips are stitched together to form a continuous loop, then placed on the quilted cushion front with right sides facing, then basted in place and machine stitched along the seam line.*

The back panel has been stitched to the front and lining, and now the cushion cover is slipped over the foam shape and the edges of the opening at the bottom are slipstitched together.

The four ties are sewn in place on the back of the cushion at each corner.

FABRIC VARIATIONS

Many different fabrics can be used for this type of cushion, producing a variety of different moods. Two alternatives are shown here. The cotton chintz features an Oriental design; this kind of print would look good with bamboo furniture, perhaps in a sun porch. The bright fruit print is cheerful and slightly humorous; something like this would suit a kitchen or a bright airy living-room decor.

*I*NSPIRATION

The technique of trapunto quilting is used worldwide, and is a good way of drawing attention to a central element in a design by making it three-dimensional on a two-dimensional background. These pages show varied examples of trapunto in both traditional and contemporary designs.

The three examples to the left all come from the Far East, and use the same trapunto technique. The central motifs – birds and elephants – have been appliquéd onto the backgrounds in contrasting fabrics, then stuffed to make them stand out from their surroundings. All of the items are richly decorated with ornate beaded embroidery, around and on top of the trapunto shapes.

This panel, called Tulips, uses trapunto quilting to highlight some of the flower petals and leaves. The three-dimensional white-on-white contrasts dramatically with the diagonal rainbow lines of embroidery and beadwork, which are echoed in the colored lines drawn on the surrounding edge.

◀ Each section in this quilt uses a different pattern of quilting, and some of the larger shapes have been padded using a variation of trapunto. Instead of stitching a pocket, which is then slit and stuffed, the designer has cut shapes of thick batting and sandwiched them in place between the quilt top and the lining. She has then quilted around the shapes, so that the back of the quilt looks as neat as the front, with no need to cover any stitched slits.

The design and color scheme of Burnt Stones, *above and right,* were inspired by different parts of Britain. The designer stitched cotton muslin by machine, then stuffed the shapes for the stones, and then dyed the piece afterwards using silk dyes.

CHAPTER 7

QUILTING AND APPLIQUÉ

Appliqué means "applied." In appliqué one fabric is stitched on top of another to produce a decorative effect.

There are several ways of combining appliqué with quilting. Some methods involve stitching the appliqué fabric to a background first and then quilting around or near it, while with other methods it's possible to use the same stitching to secure the appliqué fabric and quilt the item at the same time.

Appliqué opens up infinite possibilities for varying the texture, color, and finish of your quilted items. With so many different fabrics available today – from the sheerest voiles to thick upholstery fabrics – it's a fascinating way to explore the creative possibilities of quilting.

+ + + **QUILTING AND APPLIQUÉ · PROJECT 1** + + +

*N*IGHTGOWN CASE

This project – a pretty way to keep your nightgown handy for bedtime – makes use of the technique known as appliqué perse, which involves applying shapes cut from printed fabric to the background. It's a very good technique to start with if you are new to appliqué, because you don't have to worry about transferring the lines of a design; you simply choose your shapes from those available in your print. To keep things simple, the quilting is done at the same time as the appliqué. The stitching is done by machine zigzag, as you need a thick band of stitching to conceal the raw edges.

Preparation

Wash and press the satin and printed fabrics.

Enlarge (see page 26) the pattern pieces to the correct size onto paper and cut them out.

Cut one of the squared shapes and two of the rectangular shapes out of the satin. Cut one squared shape from the muslin and one from the batting.

Quilting

1 Choose the part of the printed pattern on the fabric that you want to use on the nightgown case, and cut it out, leaving a ½–¾ in (1.5–2 cm) margin all around.

2 Iron transfer fusing web onto the back of the shape.

3 Using the embroidery scissors, cut around the motif, leaving a margin of about ¹⁄₁₆ in (2 mm) all around the edges.

4 Peel off the backing paper, and position the motif on the front of the satin square. When you are happy with the

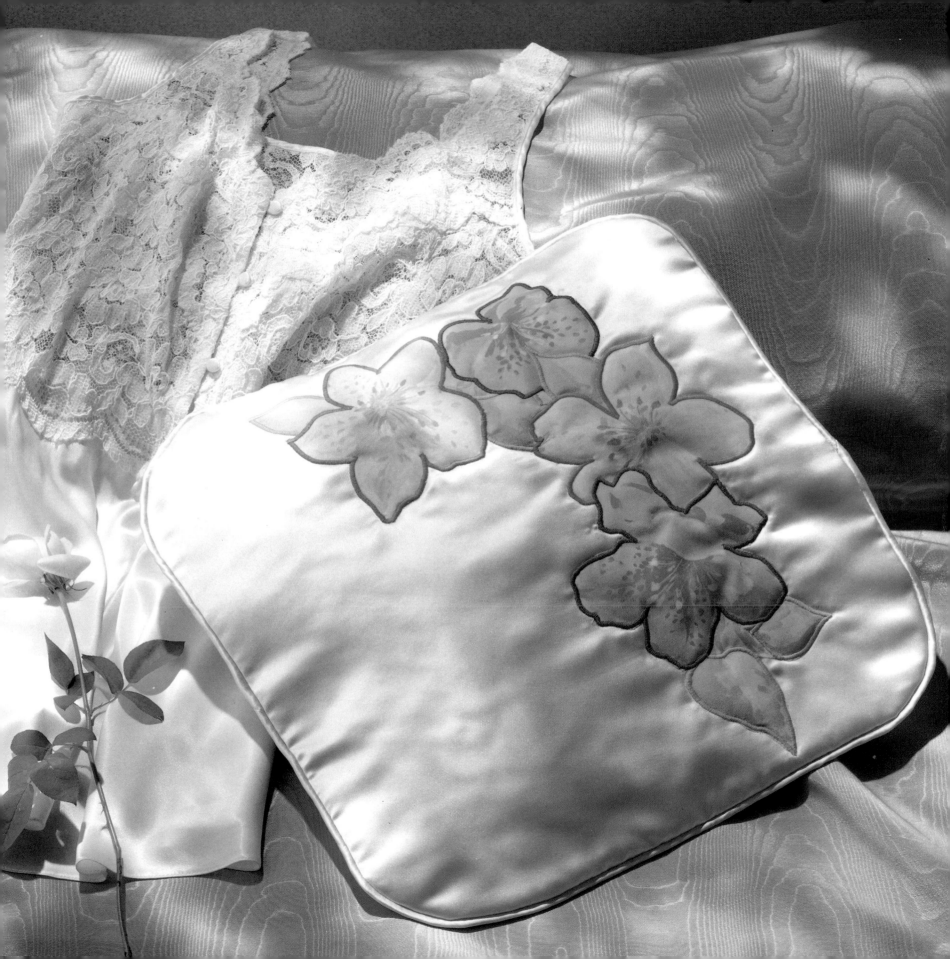

MATERIALS

1 piece of peach satin at least 20 in (50 cm) long and 40 in (1 m) wide (plus extra if you want to cord the edges of the nightgown case)

Scraps of printed fabric in harmonizing colors

Sewing *or* machine embroidery threads to match the main colors of the printed fabric

1 piece of lightweight polyester batting 18 in (46 cm) square

1 piece of muslin the same size as the batting

2¼ yd (2 m) medium filler cord, if cording

Scraps of transfer fusing web

Thread to match the satin

Very sharp embroidery scissors

Pattern for case front

positioning, iron the motif onto the satin to bond it in place.

5 Place the muslin on a flat surface and put the batting on top. Lay the satin square, right side up, on top of the batting, and baste all three layers together around the edges of the motif, adding extra lines of basting if the fabrics need it.

6 Using a close zigzag or satin stitch, stitch around the edges of the main lines of the motif, matching the colors of the threads to the colors on the printed fabric.

7 Remove the basting threads, and press the design gently on the wrong side.

Finishing

8 Press under and stitch a double hem along the long straight edges of the satin rectangles.

9 If you are cording the edges, cut bias strips from the extra satin, join them, and baste them over the cord (see page 19).

10 Lay the quilted square right side up on a flat surface, and position the rectangles face down over the top so that the hemmed edges overlap down the middle. (If you are using cording, insert

1¼ in
(3.2 cm)

Quilting *An attractively shaped motif is cut from the printed fabric, leaving a generous margin around the edges.*

Transfer fusing web is ironed onto the back of the fabric shape, then the edges of the fabric are trimmed close to the outline of the motif.

The backing paper is peeled away from the back of the motif.

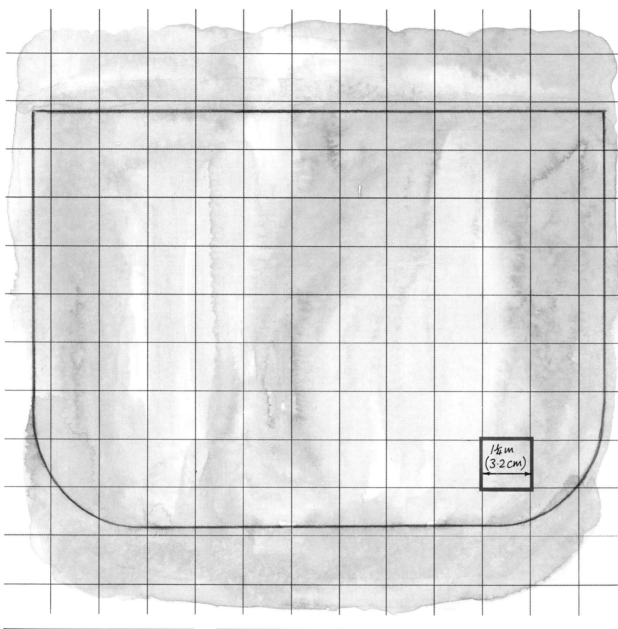

1¼ in
(3·2 cm)

Pattern for nightgown case back

it between the layers around the outside edges at this stage.) Pin and baste around the edges for a ¼ in (5 mm) seam, and machine stitch along this line twice for strength.

11 Turn the nightgown case right side out, and press it gently.

Variations

Simply choosing a different color for the satin background creates quite a different effect, as does a bright, firm cotton.

The same pattern can be used to make a square cushion cover – simply cut the pattern shapes with square corners instead of rounded ones, and put a pillow form of the appropriate size inside when the stitching has been completed. You don't have to use one large motif for the design on the front either. You can cut smaller ones and scatter them over the front of the satin. Individual motifs – for example, several flowers and leaves – can be cut from the fabric then built up into one large pattern; simply iron them in position, overlapping them if necessary, and the fusing web will keep them in place.

TIPS FOR PROFESSIONAL RESULTS

● When you stitch around the design, make sure that you stitch over any raw edges where two pieces are joined, and then when the stitching is finished no one will realize that there is a seam underneath. It also gives a much smoother effect than if the edges of the shapes are turned under before stitching.

The motif is positioned on the front of the satin square and ironed in place.

The satin square, batting and muslin are basted together around the motif, then the main outlines of the motif are stitched over with machine zigzag or satin stitch in the matching colors.

The front, backing pieces and cording are stitched together in one seam, and then the nightgown case is turned right side out.

QUILTING AND APPLIQUÉ · PROJECT 2

+ + +   + + +

*B*RIGHT RUG

Even large shapes can be decorated with quilting and appliqué, as this rug shows.

The bright primary colors against the white background give it a very "modern art" look. The appliqué itself is straightforward, but the secret of success lies in the accurate cutting and positioning of the colored pieces on the background, which is helped by using transfer fusing web.

Choose a durable upholstery fabric for the background, so that it will stand up to wear and tear, and when the rug becomes grubby, it can be easily washed on a gentle machine program.

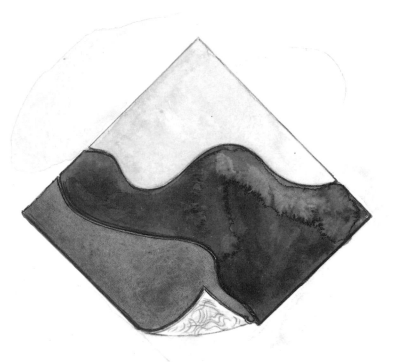

Preparation

Wash and press all the fabrics (check that all the colored fabrics are colorfast).

On the paper side of the fusing web, draw 18 boxes – each 7½ in (19 cm) square – and cut them out.

Draw wiggly lines in pencil to sepa-

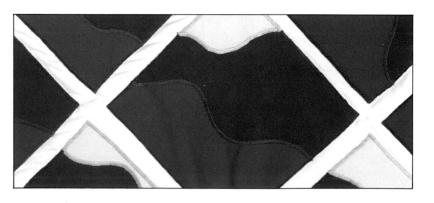

Preparation *Having been backed with fusing web, the fabric pieces are laid on the background fabric in their squares, with the edges of the pieces abutting; they are then ironed in place.*

MATERIALS

2 pieces of strong white fabric, each 40 x 50 in (1 x 1.3 m)
1 piece of extra-thick batting the same size as the white fabric
1 piece of yellow fabric 39 x 43–44 in (100 x 110–112 cm)
1 piece of blue fabric (20–30 x 43–44 in (50–75 x 110–112 cm)
1 piece of red fabric the same size as the blue fabric
2 spools each of machine embroidery thread in blue, red, and yellow
White sewing thread
Transfer fusing web – about 2 sq yd (2 sq m)

rate each square into three areas. You don't need to be too careful with the lines – let them flow freely – but remember that the shapes will be reversed when they are cut out of fabric.

Arrange the fusing web squares in the pattern shown in the rug chart, altering the order they are in until you are happy with the balance of the design. Then mark each square with a number (1 through 18) to designate its position in the layout.

On the back of the squares, mark each separate section with a number and a letter to denote the square it belongs to and the color fabric you will use for it. So, for example, square 1 will be divided into three sections: 1Y for the piece that will be yellow, 1R for the piece that will be red, and 1B for the piece that will be blue, and so on. Work down from yellow, through red, to blue,

on each square.

Cut along the wiggly lines to separate the pieces, and group them into three piles by their color codes.

Iron all the yellow pieces onto the back of the yellow fabric, and repeat the process with the red pieces and fabric and the blue pieces and fabric. Cut out the fabric pieces, but don't peel off the paper.

Reassemble the squares on the background fabric in the original order. You should now have 18 squares, each made up from a yellow section, a red section, and a blue section, arranged evenly on your background fabric.

Working on one square at a time, peel off the backing papers and carefully reposition the pieces on the background, abutting their edges. Iron them to bond them to the background fabric. Repeat the process until all the shapes are fused in place.

Quilting

1 Thread your machine with one color, and use a wide satin stitch or close zigzag to stitch around all the fabric sections of that color. Repeat with the remaining two colors. When the stitching is complete, press the work thoroughly.

2 Lay the other piece of white fabric on a flat surface, and lay the batting on top of it. Position the appliquéd fabric on top of the batting, and secure all the layers together with regular lines of basting stitches, crisscrossing between the diamonds.

3 Set your machine to a long straight stitch ⅛ in (3–4 mm), thread it with the white thread, and stitch across the quilt diagonally so that the lines of stitching run close to each edge of each diamond. Continue the lines of stitching out to the edges of the fabric.

4 Remove the basting threads.

Finishing

5 Cut 4 in (10 cm) strips of the remaining yellow fabric to fit the sides and ends of the rug, with 1 in (2.5 cm) extra at each end (join the fabric to form the strips if necessary).

Pattern for bright rug

Quilting The raw edges of the shapes are stitched along in satin or close zigzag stitching using threads matching the colors.

The applied fabric, batting, and backing fabric are basted together, then quilted by machine in long straight lines of stitching worked diagonally across the rug, using the edges of the squares as stitching guides.

TIPS FOR PROFESSIONAL RESULTS

• When you have laid the colored pieces onto the fabric in a pleasing arrangement, mark the corners of each square with a dot in water-soluble pen. This will make the final positioning of the pieces easier and more accurate as you iron them on.

• If you're not confident about stitching straight lines across the quilt, mark them with water-soluble or fading pen first, then, after stitching, use a damp cloth to remove any visible marks.

6 Cut some strips of the remaining blue and red fabric the same width, and back them with transfer fusing web.

7 Cut the red and blue strips into random lengths with wiggly lines, and position them in a pleasing arrangement on the yellow strips. Keep the fabric colors in the same sequence all the way around, and use the red or blue fabric to cover any seams in the yellow strips. Peel off the backing papers, and then iron the pieces to bond them firmly to the yellow fabric.

8 Stitch along the wavy lines in the appropriate-colored thread, using satin or close zigzag stitching.

9 Use the decorated strips to bind the edges of the rug (see page 16). The machine stitching creates a quilted border around the edges of the rug.

Variations

If you don't like or don't want the extra work of the multicolored border, sim-

Finishing Random shapes of red and blue fabric are applied to the yellow edging strips, again being stitched with thread of a matching color.

ply bind the rug with the white fabric, or choose just one of the colors from the main pattern.

For more variety in the pattern, you can mix the order in which the colors appear, changing them around at the stage when you are coding the fusing web pieces.

If bright primaries don't fit in with your color scheme, choose a neutral background fabric, and pick up the colors of your carpet and curtains or draperies in the appliquéd pieces.

You can use printed fabrics for the appliqué, too, but choose designs that are small or subtle, otherwise it can look too busy. If you do want to use a fabric with a bigger design, use whole squares instead of making each square from three different fabrics.

QUILTING AND APPLIQUÉ · PROJECT 3

+ + +   + + +

QUILTED PLAY MAT

Every child loves a special place to play with their toys, and this play mat is ideal. The design includes roads, railroads, paths, water, and favorite items such as a bandstand and an ice-cream stand, so there's plenty of opportunity for varied play.

Use as many different fabrics for the appliqué as possible, so that you have a variety of textures and colors. This is an excellent way to use up all those scraps of fabric in your sewing chest, for almost no scrap is too small to be incorporated somewhere into the design.

Each fabric piece is backed with transfer fusing web, then the appliqué and quilting are done together by machine.

Preparation

Wash and press the green and white fabrics and other cotton scraps that you intend to use.

Tape together several large pieces of paper and enlarge (see page 26) the play mat design to the correct size.

On the front of the fusing web, trace the shapes required for the pathways across the park. Cut the shapes out, iron them onto the back of the beige fabric, and cut around the shapes.

Peel off the backing paper, position the pieces of beige fabric on the right side of the green fabric, and iron to bond them in place.

Repeat these last two steps with the shapes and fabrics for the pond, the hedges, and the road.

Gradually work through all the medium-sized elements of the design, positioning the larger ones (such as the bandstand roof) first, then the smaller ones, and iron them all into place.

Finish with the smallest pieces of fabric, such as the deckchair struts, and the crossties for the railroad line.

Quilting

1 Lay the white backing fabric on a flat surface, and put the layers of batting on top, smoothing them out. Lay the fabric with the appliquéd picture on it, right side up, on top of the batting. Baste through all four layers at regular intervals in order to hold them together so that they are flat.

2 Set the machine to zigzag, and use the

MATERIALS

1 piece of light green cotton or polyester-cotton fabric 39 in (1 m) square

1 piece of white fabric the same size as the green fabric

2 layers of thick batting the same size as the green fabric

4 strips of blue fabric, each 6 in (15 cm) wide and 39 in (1 m) long

Large scraps of beige, pale blue, gray, and medium-green fabric

Lots of small scraps of fabrics in bright colors, solid and printed

Transfer fusing web – about 1/2–1 sq yd (1/2–1 sq m)

Sewing thread in a neutral color

TIPS FOR APPLIQUÉ QUILTED PICTURES

● Some printed fabrics suggest ideas for appliqué – especially for light-hearted projects such as play mats – and are ideal if you are lacking inspiration for a design! Look for fabrics that already contain pictures and shapes that can be cut out and used if you'd rather not draw your own.

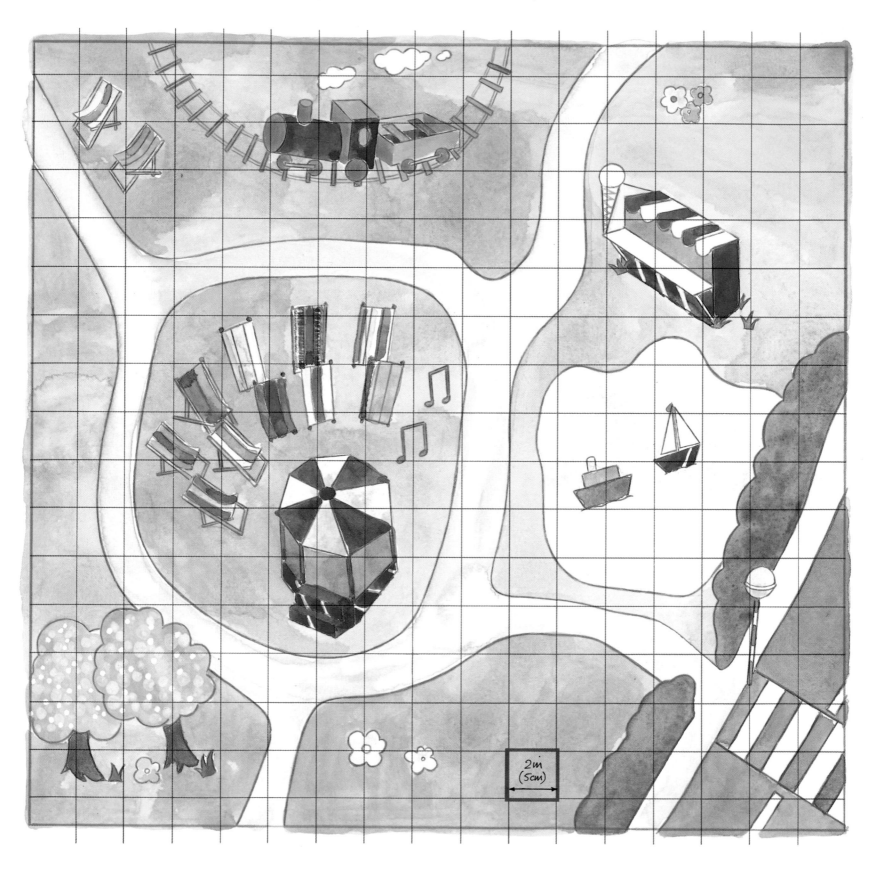

2in
(5cm)

Design for the play mat

same color thread to quilt around each of the pieces. Vary the size of the stitches a little to suit the size of the piece you are appliquéing. Begin quilting from the center outward, stitching all the large areas first, then, starting at the center again, stitch round all the small areas. Lines such as the railroad tracks can be made from lines of zigzag or satin stitch in an appropriate thread color.

3 When the stitching is complete, remove the basting threads.

Finishing

4 Trim the edges of the play mat by about 1 in (2.5 cm) on all sides. Bind the edges of the quilt with the strips of blue fabric (see page 16), attaching the top and bottom pieces first, then the two side pieces.

Variations

A play mat can be made with scenes other than the park given here. Why not try designing your own pattern based on a zoo, the beach, or your own garden? Or adapt the basic design here to include other features that mean something to your child – a farm or a playground.

This kind of appliqué quilt can also be used to make a kicking mat for a baby – appliqué some bright-colored animals (perhaps cut out of printed fabric) or alphabet blocks.

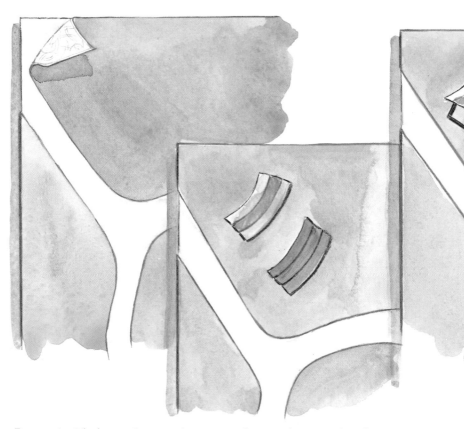

Preparation *The largest shapes, such as the pathways, are backed with transfer fusing web, then ironed in place on the background fabric before the other pieces.*

Medium-sized pieces such as the deckchairs and the bandstand follow next, using exactly the same technique.

Finally, the smallest details, the deckchair struts and the railroad crossties, are added to the design and ironed in place.

TIPS FOR PROFESSIONAL RESULTS

- Very tiny bits of fabric tend to fall off while the larger pieces are being quilted, so you may find it useful to secure them to the background with a single stitch while you are working on the other areas.

- Quilting the small, shaped areas, such as the flowers, can be a bit tricky, so turn the machine speed to slow, and manipulate the fabric carefully so that you stitch smoothly around the edges.

- Finish off each line of stitching by pulling the threads through to the back and knotting them; this gives a neater finish on the right side than reversing over the ends.

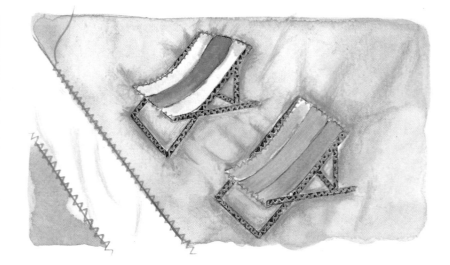

Quilting *Once all the fabric pieces are securely in place, the raw edges are stitched along with machine zigzag stitching – one color of thread being used for most of the shapes.*

QUILTING AND APPLIQUÉ · PROJECT 4

STAINED GLASS QUILT

The spectacular colors and lines of modern stained glass inspired this design, which works its way through a rainbow selection of solid-colored and printed fabrics.

The technique used is sometimes also known as stained glass *patchwork,* but it is actually an appliqué technique.

The lines made by the strips of black bias binding imitate the leading in stained glass windows. Using bias binding makes it possible to curve the lines easily to follow the bright shapes underneath.

Preparation

Wash and press all the fabrics you are going to use.

Tape together several large sheets of paper (brown paper or newspaper will do, but white is easier to use) to cover the area of one piece of the sheeting. Divide this area into 10 in (25 cm) squares with pencil lines, and enlarge the chart onto it (see page 26). Go over all the curves of the quilt design with the thick black felt-tip pen.

Place the chart flat on the floor, and tape one of the pieces of sheeting over it. Trace over the curved lines from the chart using either the soft pencil or tailor's chalk (all these lines will be covered by fabric and tape, so don't worry about their showing).

Mark clearly on the chart which pieces you want in which colors. You can either work through the rainbow, with the patterned fabrics down the center as in the photograph; or position the colors at random.

Starting at the top of the chart, cut out several pieces, and use them as templates for cutting the appropriate fabrics. Position these fabrics within the lines on the marked piece of sheeting. (It is best to do just a few pieces at a time, otherwise you will soon lose track of which piece goes where.)

When you have cut and positioned all the fabric pieces, check that you are happy with the pattern made by the colors. If you are not and there are any you want to change, re-cut them in different fabrics now.

Quilting

1 When your design is complete, pin each piece of fabric in position and then carefully and loosely roll up the sheeting. Lay out the other piece of sheeting, position the batting on top, then gently unroll the pinned design over the batting.

2 Check that all the edges of the layers are even, then baste all three layers together with regular rows of basting across the width of the quilt.

3 Cut appropriate lengths of the narrow bias binding, and position them, one at a time, over where the fabric pieces join, straddling the two pieces of fabric evenly. Curve the binding gently to follow the curve of the marked line. Pin and baste each piece of binding down both edges so that the raw edges of fabric are firmly trapped. Continue until all the black tapes are in position.

4 Thread your sewing machine with the black thread, and set it to a medium-length straight stitch (about 1/8 in [3 mm]). Machine stitch along both edges of each strip of bias binding, stitching the inside of each curve first. With this method the quilting and appliqué are thus done simultaneously. Where one bias strip crosses another, simply stitch across the joint.

5 Remove all the basting threads once all the tape has been stitched down.

MATERIALS

2 pieces of white cotton or polyester-cotton sheeting, each 60 x 90 in (150 x 230 cm)

1 piece of lightweight polyester batting the same size as the sheeting

Mixed solid and printed fabrics in bright colors – you will need about 6 sq yd (6 sq m)

Black bias binding 1 in (2.5 cm) wide and about 55 yd (50 m) long

Black bias binding 2 in (5 cm) wide and 10 yd (9 m) long

2 spools black machine embroidery thread, *or* similar

Thick black felt-tip pen

Soft pencil *or* tailor's chalk

90in
(228cm)

60in
(152cm)

TIPS FOR PROFESSIONAL RESULTS

● Buy a "bed size" piece of batting so that you don't have to join two or more widths.

● For the sake of economy, contact a wholesale notions dealer, and see if you can buy the bias binding you need wholesale, or make your own bias strips from black fabric.

● Make sure that you stitch the inside edge of each curve *before* the outside edge, as this prevents the binding from stretching too much as it is stitched.

● Adjoining pieces of the same color can be cut out together as one piece of fabric – you don't need to cut down the line between them.

● When you come to stitching the black tapes near the center of the design, roll the right-hand side of the quilt up tightly so that it will fit under the arm of the sewing machine.

Chart for the stained glass quilt

Finishing

6 Bind the edges of the quilt with the wide bias binding (see page 17).

Variations

Many different solid-colored or printed fabrics can be used to stunning effect with this technique. Instead of using bright cotton fabrics, you can substitute pastels or shades of just a few colors, or even satins or metallic fabrics. The leading doesn't *have* to be black – you might choose instead to pick out one of the colors from your fabrics.

The two samples of stained glass appliqué shown here demonstrate just how different a pattern can look depending on the fabrics used. Exactly the same pattern has been used for cutting the fabric pieces and positioning the bias binding.

Glitter is the watchword for this first example. The fabrics used are white and pale pink satin, and silver, bright pink, and silver/pink metallic fabrics. The leading has been made with gray satin bias binding (the sheen of the satin making it look silver), stitched down with metallic thread.

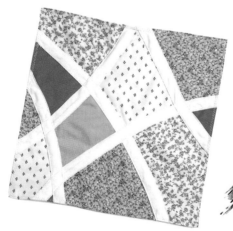

In total contrast, this example captures an English country cottage style. The fabrics are all cottons in blue and cream prints and solid colors, and the leading has been made with bias strips cut from a matching cream fabric.

Preparation *The pattern pieces are cut out of the different fabrics, using the enlarged chart as a cutting guide, then laid in position within the lines marked on the background fabric.*

Quilting *Once all the fabric pieces are in position and the quilt top has been basted to the batting and backing, the black bias binding is pinned along the lines where the fabric pieces meet, the joint running down the center of the bias binding strips.*

Using machine straight stitch, both edges of the bias binding are stitched down, trapping the raw edges of the fabric pieces underneath them and quilting at the same time.

INSPIRATION

Appliqué is a very versatile craft, and as the examples on this page show, it can be used to stunning effect when teamed up with quilting. If your finished item needs to be hardwearing, the raw edges of the fabric must be firmly stitched, but if your creation is purely decorative, anything goes!

Appliqué perse was used for this Green Apples *jacket; scraps of printed fabric were cut to shape then appliquéd onto a black background, padded, and quilted with metallic thread. Bugle beads and tiny insect beads add the final touches.*

Blue/green iridescent silk was used for this panel, entitled Under the Shadow of His Wings. *Gold Lurex shapes were basted onto the feathers in a random pattern, then the whole piece was stitched over in metallic threads in various colors. The border is imitation gold kid.*

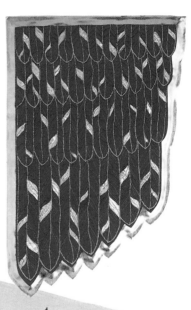

▶ *Fleurs-de-lys, stars, and squares cut from red fabric decorate this English quilt, signed "Lissy Dixon, Nov. 14, 1938". A separate signature simply says "Luther". Maybe her son, Luther, helped to cut out the fabric shapes.*

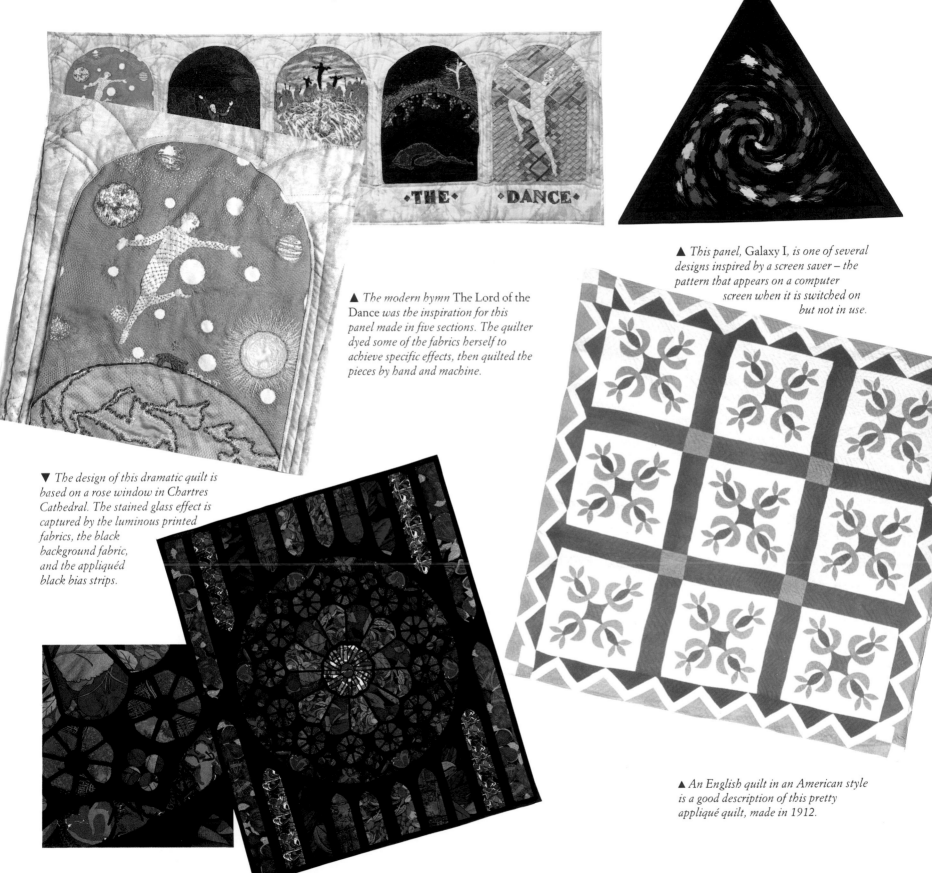

▲ *This panel, Galaxy I, is one of several designs inspired by a screen saver – the pattern that appears on a computer screen when it is switched on but not in use.*

▲ *The modern hymn* The Lord of the Dance *was the inspiration for this panel made in five sections. The quilter dyed some of the fabrics herself to achieve specific effects, then quilted the pieces by hand and machine.*

▼ *The design of this dramatic quilt is based on a rose window in Chartres Cathedral. The stained glass effect is captured by the luminous printed fabrics, the black background fabric, and the appliquéd black bias strips.*

▲ *An English quilt in an American style is a good description of this pretty appliqué quilt, made in 1912.*

CHAPTER 8

QUILTING AND PATCHWORK

We're all familiar with the term "patchwork quilt". This form of bedcover has, for centuries, been the most popular way of combining the skills of quilting and patchwork.

There are, however, many other ways of putting the two skills together, and this chapter looks at just some of the possibilities. Generally the fabric pieces for the patchwork are joined, or "pieced", before being quilted, but some techniques allow you to do the two jobs together. You can quilt either in, or alongside, the seams in the patchwork, or you can stitch an independent quilting pattern around or across the patchwork, perhaps reflecting or repeating one of the shapes of the pieced fabrics.

+ + + **QUILTING AND PATCHWORK · PROJECT 1** + + +

The traditional Christmas tree is here interpreted in a padded patchwork shape for this hanging Christmas decoration. Choose as many different Christmassy fabrics as possible (many quilting retailers sell packs containing small pieces of suitable fabrics), or choose solids and prints in combinations of red, green, and white.

The pattern is very easy and makes a good project for newcomers to patchwork. The triangles are pieced by hand or by machine before being quilted.

MATERIALS

Scraps of 19 different cotton or polyester-cotton fabrics in Christmassy colors and/or patterns
Ready-made bow *or* green satin ribbon (20 in [50 cm]) tied into a bow
Green bias binding 1 in (2.5 cm) wide and 2 yd (2 m) long
Piece of thick batting 20 in (50 cm) square
Piece of solid red or green backing fabric, the same size as the batting
Red sewing thread
Piece of cardboard large enough to trace triangle onto
Soft pencil

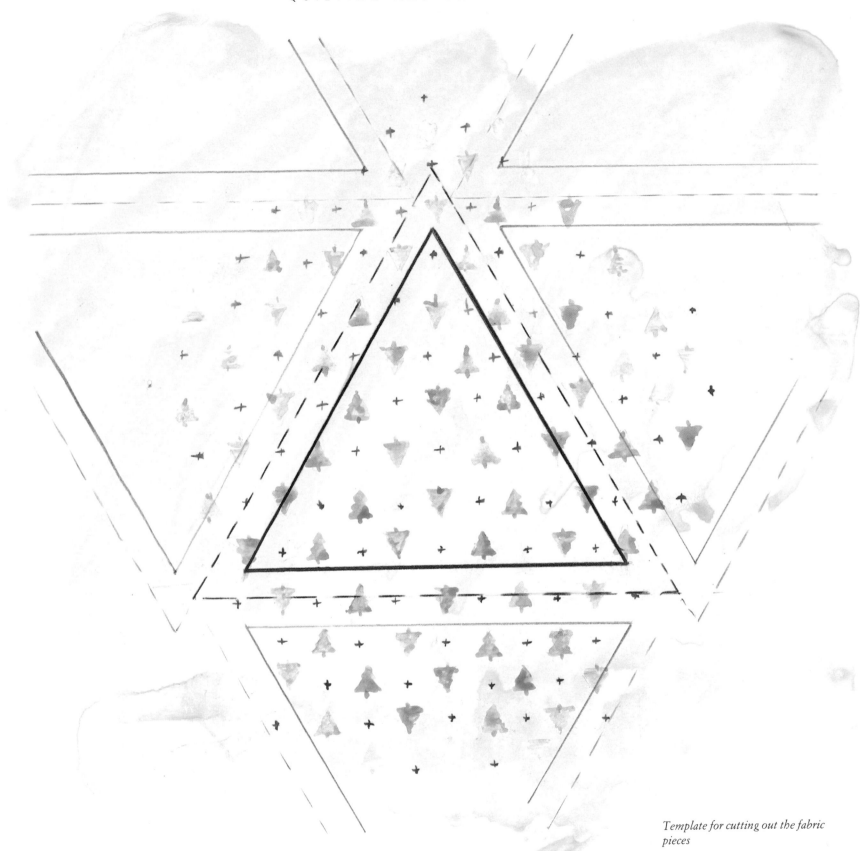

Template for cutting out the fabric pieces

TIPS FOR PROFESSIONAL RESULTS

• If you can't find 19 different fabrics that are suitable, cut several patches from the same fabric and scatter them through the design.

• To make it easier to match the seams accurately when you are joining the rows, put the point of a pin through one side of the seam where the triangle tips meet, then put it through the same place on the other side and push them together. This will match them up exactly; you can then baste the seam so that it will stay in place for stitching.

Preparation

Trace the triangle onto a piece of cardboard and cut it out carefully. This is your template for the patchwork pieces.

Press all the fabrics that you will be using.

Draw around the template on the back of each fabric scrap using a soft pencil. Cut out the shapes, leaving a ⅜ in (1 cm) seam allowance all around the pencil lines.

Arrange the fabric triangles in a pleasing pattern, following the shape of the Christmas tree in the photograph.

Stitch the triangles into rows across the shape; first pin and baste each seam together, then stitch by hand or machine along the pencil lines. Press each seam open before you stitch the next.

Trim off any excess fabric from the edges of the seams (but not too close to the seams themselves), and stitch the rows together to form the tree shape. Press the seams open and trim at the edges of the tree shape.

Quilting

1 Cut the batting and the backing fabric to the shape of the pieced tree.
2 Lay the backing fabric right side down on a flat surface, and put the batting on top. Place the pieced tree, right side up, over the batting, and baste all three layers together with several rows of basting stitches.
3 If you are quilting by machine, set your sewing machine to a medium-length straight stitch ¹⁄₁₆ in (2 mm) and use the red thread to stitch along the lines of the seams to quilt the shape.

If you are quilting by hand, use the red thread and quilt along the seam lines using running stitch or backstitch.

Finishing

4 Edge the shape with the green bias binding (see page 17), and sew the bow in place at the top of the "pot."
5 Sew small loops onto the back of the decoration, or just one at the top so that it can be hung up.

Variations

If you want to make the quilted lines more obvious, thread your sewing machine with green or red, and stitch along the seamlines of the triangles with satin stitch or close zigzag instead of straight stitch.

For a really glitzy effect, make the shape in glittery and metallic fabrics in different colors.

If you can find ribbon printed with a Christmas design, you might want to use it for making the bow instead of using a solid color.

Preparation The triangles are marked on the back of the fabrics and cut out, adding a seam allowance all around, then laid out to form a pleasing arrangement.

They are then stitched into rows and the seams pressed open.

The rows of triangles are stitched to each other to produce a tree shape, with the seamlines matched carefully, then the seams are pressed open.

Quilting The batting and backing fabric are cut to shape, then basted together with the patchwork shape on top. Each seamline is quilted with a straight line of red machine stitching.

QUILTING AND PATCHWORK · PROJECT 2

STRIPED JERKIN

The bright jerkin shown here makes use of a variation of the technique known as "quilt as you go." The seams that join the strips of colored fabric quilt the garment at the same time.

This is an ideal project for using up small scraps of fabric, making them into a garment that will delight a young child, but be sure to choose fabrics that are of similar weights and fibers.

The pattern given here fits a child aged about 6, but you could scale it up or down slightly for a younger or older child.

Seams are kept to a minimum, and the edges are finished with bias binding in a selection of colors that harmonize with the stripes.

Make the jerkin extra useful by choosing colors that match outfits already in the child's wardrobe.

Jerkin pattern

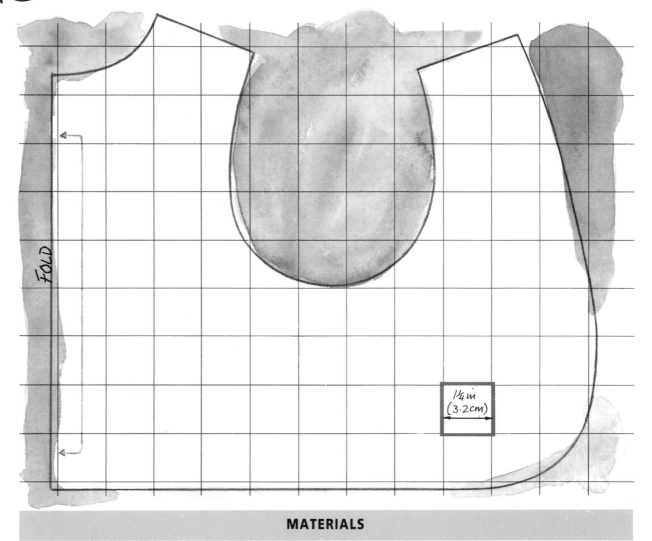

MATERIALS

1 piece of white cotton or polyester-cotton fabric 15 x 30 in (38 x 76 cm)
1 piece of muslin the same size as the white fabric
1 piece of thick polyester batting the same size as the white fabric
Scraps of plain cotton or polyester-cotton fabric in bright colors (as a guide, you will need scraps that cover about twice the area of the jerkin pattern, to allow for seams and for positioning colors where you want them)
3 pieces of bias binding in bright colors, each 1½ in (4 cm) wide: 1 x 62 in (160 cm) long and 2 x 20 in (50 cm) long
Matching sewing threads
White sewing thread

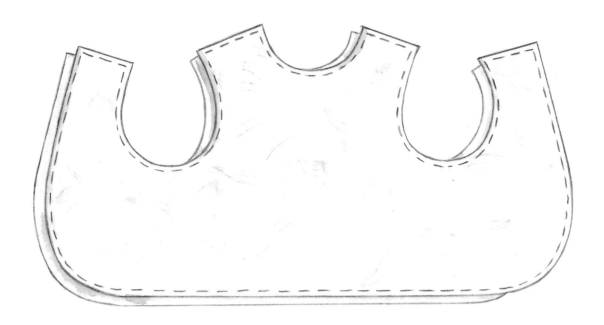

Preparation *The lining, batting, and muslin are cut to shape, and the batting* *is then basted to the muslin in order to hold the two layers together during* *quilting.*

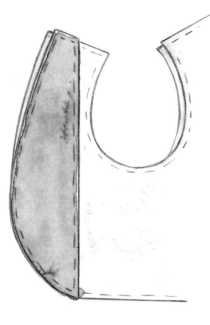 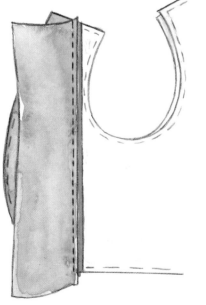 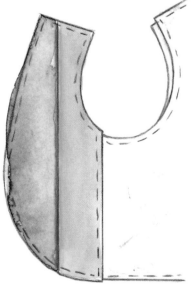

Quilting *The first strip of fabric is cut to the required width, then basted, right side up, to the left-hand edge of the jerkin shape. It is then trimmed to fit.*

The next strip of fabric is cut to the required width and placed face down over the first strip, and the right-hand edges are stitched down.

The new strip of fabric is folded over to the right, basted in place, and then trimmed to shape along the top and bottom.

Preparation

Enlarge (see page 26) the jerkin pattern to the correct size, and cut the shape out of paper.

Wash and press all the fabrics you will be using.

Fold the white fabric in half across its width, place the "fold" edge of the pattern along the fold, and cut out the fabric to produce the jerkin shape. Do the same with the muslin and batting.

Place the muslin shape on a flat surface, and position the batting on top. Baste the two pieces together with lines of close basting stitches across the shapes and around the edges.

Quilting

1 Choose a color for your first strip and cut the fabric to the desired width, adding ¼ in (5 mm) seam allowance along one of the long edges. With the batting face up, baste the fabric strip, right side up, along the far left side of the jerkin shape, and trim it so that it follows the curve.

2 Choose a fabric for your next strip and cut it to the desired width, adding ¼ in (5 mm) at both sides for seams. Place it right side down over the first strip, lining up the right-hand edges, and baste it down ¼ in (5 mm) from the edges. Stitch along this line in machine straight stitch, or in close running stitches if sewing by hand.

3 Fold the strip over to the right, so that it is now right side up, and trim the top and bottom to the shape of the batting and muslin if necessary.

4 Continue in the same way across the jerkin shape, varying the colors and widths of the strips to make an attractive design. Make sure that you keep each strip vertical.

5 When you have completed the final strip, fold it over to the right, as before, and baste it down. Stitch around all the raw edges of the jerkin shape, very close to the edge, with a line of straight machine stitching.

Finishing

6 With right sides together, join the shoulder seams of the jerkin, taking a very narrow seam allowance.

7 Stitch the shoulder seams of the lining fabric in the same way.

8 With wrong sides together, baste the lining inside the jerkin shape 1 in (2.5 cm) from the raw edges.

9 Bind the armholes and the other raw edges of the jerkin with the bias binding (see page 17).

Variations

Choose solid-colored fabrics in a range of pastel shades if you want a more subtle effect, or select harmonizing prints and solid colors.

If you prefer, you can finish the edges in the same color of bias binding instead of using three different colors.

For a special occasion such as a party or a wedding, you could make a jerkin for a little girl in pastel satins or pinwale corduroy – perhaps to match a party dress.

Finishing The raw edges are bound with bias binding in three different colors.

TIPS FOR PROFESSIONAL RESULTS

• If you aren't confident about stitching your seams straight, mark the seam allowances on the edges of the fabric strips in soft pencil or tailor's chalk.

• If the weave in your fabrics is straight, you can produce straight strips by making a small nick in the edge of each fabric and tearing it down the grain.

Quilting and finishing When the patchwork is complete, a line of stitching is worked along all the raw edges to hold the layers together firmly. The jerkin shape is folded, with the

right sides together, and the shoulders are joined in a narrow seam.

Finishing The shoulder seams of the lining are joined in the same way, and the lining is basted inside the patchwork, wrong sides together.

The stripes here are made from solid and printed cotton fabrics in white, several shades of blue and pale pink. All the prints used are floral, but you could use a mixture of different designs. Don't vary them too much, though, as

the striped patchwork is a very strong pattern in its own right. For the same reason, it's best to choose small prints – larger ones have too many distracting lines.

Instead of bright colors, this example uses solid-colored fabrics in pastel shades, giving a more subtle striped effect. You can achieve this effect with cotton or polyester-cotton fabrics or with pastel silks or satins.

QUILTING AND PATCHWORK · PROJECT 3

SHOULDER BAG

Black and white fabrics in all kinds of patterns have been combined in this project to produce a jazzy piece of patchwork that forms the centerpiece for a striking shoulder bag. The patchwork shapes are highlighted with small triangles of red, and the red is picked up in the quilting bars and in the colored stripe on the bag handle.

Although the patchwork shape looks complicated, it is easily stitched by machine in a series of straight seams – all you need to do is follow the correct stitching order for the seams and the pattern will form itself.

Preparation The patchwork pieces are cut from the fabric, and laid out to check they look right together. All the seams marked A in the chart are stitched to begin building up the pattern.

after every stage so that they lie flat.

When the patchwork square is complete, check that all the sides are even and straight (trim them slightly if they are uneven).

Cut 3 in (8 cm) wide strips from the remaining black fabric, join them to the top and bottom of the patchwork square in ⅜ in (1 cm) seams, and press them open.

Join two more strips to the sides of the square in the same way, and press the seams open. You should now have a square measuring 18 in (46 cm) on all

MATERIALS

1 piece of strong black fabric (twill, serge, sailcloth) 36 x 43 in (1 x 1.10 m)

2 squares of thick polyester batting 18 in (46 cm) square

2 pieces of muslin the same size as the batting

Scraps of black and white printed cotton fabrics

Small scraps of solid red cotton fabric

Red ribbon or seam binding 1 in (2.5 cm) wide and 1 yd (1 m) long

2 spools of machine embroidery thread in scarlet

Black sewing thread

Soft pencil or tailor's chalk

Preparation

Wash and press all the fabrics.

Enlarge (see page 26) the patchwork chart to the correct size on stiff paper, and number the pieces as shown in the chart. Write under the number a description of the fabric that you think will look best in that area, e.g., 1, thick stripes. Then cut the pattern into pieces along the straight lines to produce a series of templates.

Cut three 18 in (46 cm) squares from the black fabric and one strip 4½ in (11 cm) wide and 1 yd (1 m) long.

Place each template face down on the wrong side of the appropriate fabric, and draw around it with a soft pencil or tailor's chalk.

Cut out each piece of fabric, adding a ⅜ in (1 cm) seam allowance along all the edges.

Lay the fabric pieces out in order, so

that you can see how the complete design looks. (If any piece doesn't look quite right, re-cut it in another fabric.)

Machine stitch all the seams marked A in the chart, using the marked lines as stitching guides. Press the seams open, and trim off any corners of fabric that stick out beyond the edges of the seam allowance.

Repeat this for the seams marked B, C, D, and E, pressing the seams open

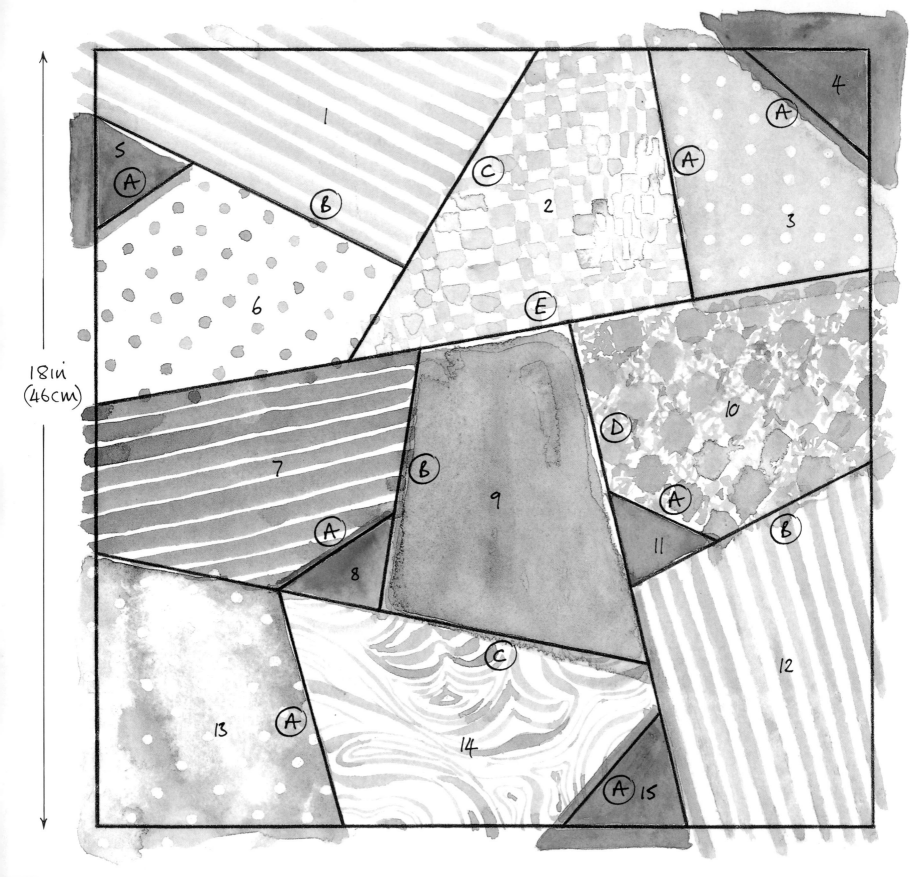

Preparation *The seams are ironed open.*

The remaining seams are stitched in order, producing a square of patchwork. Any uneven edges are trimmed.

Preparation and quilting *The black border is added to the square, then the patchwork bag front is basted to the layers of batting and muslin. Long bars*

of machine satin stitch or close zigzag are stitched in scarlet thread along each seamline and around the inside of the border.

Chart for the bag

sides; if it is a little bigger, trim it slightly all the way around so that the borders are even.

Quilting

1 Place one of the pieces of muslin on a flat surface and put one square of the batting on top. Cover the batting with the patchwork square, right side up, and baste the layers together with several close rows of basting stitches.

2 Set your sewing machine to satin or close zigzag stitch ³⁄₁₆ in (4 mm) wide and thread it with the red thread. Quilt the patchwork by working long bars of stitching along the seamlines, quilting the seams in the same order that you pieced them (follow the order marked on the chart). This will insure that the ends of each stitching line will be covered by the next bar.

3 Finish the quilting by working satin stitch or close zigzag along the seams between the central square and the outer black strips.

Finishing

4 Place the second square of muslin on a flat surface and cover with the second square of batting and one of the black squares, right side up. (If you wish, you

can quilt a design by machine on the back of the bag at this stage.)

5 Place the bag back and front together with right sides facing, and pin and baste ³⁄₈ in (1 cm) in from the sides and bottom. Stitch twice along the seamline in straight machine stitching.

6 Clip the corners and trim the raw edges of the batting and muslin close to the seamline.

7 Fold the 1 yd (1 m) long strip of black fabric in half along its length, right sides together. Baste and stitch a ¼ in (5 mm) seam along its length, then turn it right side out and press it flat to make the strap.

8 Baste the red ribbon or seam binding down the center of one side of the band, and stitch it in place with a line of straight machine stitching down each edge.

9 Place the remaining two squares of fabric together with right sides facing, and stitch a ³⁄₈ in (1 cm) seam down each side to make the lining.

10 Turn the quilted bag right side out and press. Slip the lining over the bag, right sides facing. Position the shoulder strap between the two layers at the sides, laying it down each side and under the bottom of the bag, wrong sides facing out, and check that it is not twisted. Shorten the strap at this stage .

11 Baste and stitch a ³⁄₈ in (1 cm) seam all around the top, then go over the seam several times where the handle ends are inserted.

12 Turn the lining out the right way, turn the ends in by ³⁄₈ in (1 cm), and stitch together at the edges by hand or by machine. Push the lining down inside the bag.

Variations

For an extra-special bag, make the back with patchwork in the same way as the front. Alternatively, make the patch-

work from harmonizing fabrics in a different color scheme, and use a suitable solid-colored fabric for the rest of the bag.

Any square patchwork block can be made into a bag in this way – try the Grandmother's Fan pattern on page 120, or choose one of the many other traditional American quilt block shapes such as Log Cabin, Courthouse Steps, Straight Furrow, or Starry Night. Your quilting retailers will have plenty of patterns, and you can explore your local library for ideas.

TIPS FOR PROFESSIONAL RESULTS

● When you are stitching the front and back of the bag together, check that the patchwork is the right way up, so that the top of the patchwork is at the top of the bag.

● The edges of the patchwork shapes will inevitably lie in different directions compared with the grain of the fabric, so

baste each seam first to make sure that you are not stretching any of the fabric shapes.

● Use the patterns of the fabrics themselves to provide extra drama in the patchwork. Plan the position of striped fabrics so that the stripes lie in different directions.

QUILTING AND PATCHWORK · PROJECT 4

*F*AN PILLOW COVER

The central square of this summery pillow cover is based on the traditional patchwork block known as Grandmother's Fan. The fan shape is made from seven yellow and green printed fabric patches stitched into a quarter circle, then appliquéd onto a solid-colored background. The fan shape is quilted in a sunburst design before the cover is assembled.

The piecing and the quilting can be done by hand or by machine – either way, there is only one curved seam, so the piecing is very simple.

Preparation

Trace templates A and B (right) onto thick paper or thin card using a soft pencil.

Wash and press all the fabrics you are going to use.

Cut one template A and six template B shapes from the printed fabrics, drawing around them with a soft pencil, and cut them out, then mark in the seam allowance in pencil on the backs.

Lay the six shape B pieces out next to each other in a fan shape, changing the

MATERIALS

1 piece of yellow background fabric
   12½ in (32 cm) square
2 pieces of yellow backing fabric, each
   11 x 17 in (28 x 44 cm)
1 piece of lightweight batting 17 in
   (44 cm) square
1 piece of muslin, or similar fabric, the
   same size as the batting
4 strips of green fabric for the border, 2
   x 2½ in (7 cm) wide and 12½ in
   (32 cm) long and 2 x 2½ in (7 cm)
   wide and 17 in (44 cm) long
Scraps of different green and yellow
   printed fabrics
1 pillow form 14 in (35 cm) square
Matching sewing threads
Soft pencil

Template A

Template B

order around until you have found the most balanced arrangement of the prints and colors.

Join the straight seams between two of the pieces, stitching along the pencil lines. Repeat for the other four pieces, and press all the seams so that they lie in the same direction.

Pin, baste, and stitch the curved seam between piece A and the inside curve of the fan shape, stitching along the pencil lines. Now press the seam toward the corner.

Turn the seam allowance to the wrong side along the long curved edge of the patchwork, and baste it in place, keeping the curve smooth.

Baste the completed fan to the corner of the yellow background fabric, and appliqué the curved edge to the background with invisible slipstitches. Press the seam flat.

Join the two shorter green strips to the sides of the yellow square with ¼ in (5 mm) seams. Press the seams toward the outside edges.

Join the two remaining strips to the top and bottom, also with ¼ in (5 mm) seams. Press the seams toward the outside edges.

Quilting

1 Place the muslin on a flat surface, position the batting on top of it, and place the pieced block, right side up, on top of the batting. Baste all three layers together with a crisscross grid of lines of basting.

2 Quilt the square along the lines shown in the diagram, using either machine straight stitch or even running stitches, then remove the basting threads.

Finishing

3 Turn under and stitch narrow double hems along one long side of each piece of backing fabric.

4 Place the quilted block, right side up, on a flat surface, and put the backing pieces, wrong side up, on top, overlapping the hemmed edges to fit the quilted square. Pin all around the edges, rounding the corners slightly. Stitch all around the edge in a ¼ in (5 mm) seam.

5 Trim and finish the raw edges, then

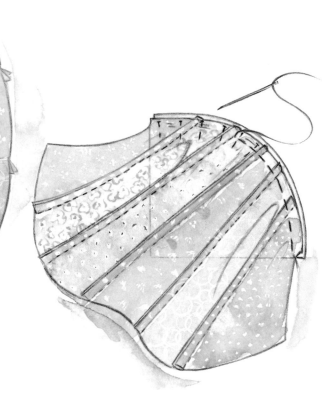

Preparation *(Top) The fan shapes are cut from the printed fabrics, arranged in a pleasing order, then stitched along the seamlines to form a quarter circle.*

(Top right) The inside fabric shape is joined to the fan with a curved seam.

(Above) The long curved edge of the patchwork is basted under, then slipstitched to the background fabric.

(Right) The patchwork shape is slipstitched to the background fabric.

turn the pillow cover right side out, press it gently, and slip the pillow form into the cover through the slit at the back.

Variations

The appearance of this quilt block can be changed totally by choosing different fabrics. If you want a bright, contemporary look, piece the fan in bright solid colors, or use strong geometric prints. For a subtle effect, piece the block in pastel-colored satins.

This block could be substituted for the black-and-white pattern on page 118, and backed with green cotton for a more rustic-looking shoulder bag.

TIPS FOR PROFESSIONAL RESULTS

• Marking the seam allowance on the pieces helps to insure that your patchwork pieces are exactly the right shape and size after seaming and will, therefore, lie fully flat, which is particularly important in complex patchwork patterns.

• Choose fabrics that are all similar in fiber content so that they lie well together – ideally all cotton fabrics, but if these are difficult to find, use all polyester-cotton blends.

• If you find it difficult to quilt in straight lines by eye, mark the lines on the fabric first with water-soluble or fading pen, and use these as stitching guides.

Preparation (Top) The green border strips are joined to the patchwork – first at the sides, then at the top and bottom.

Quilting (Above) The muslin, batting, and patchwork block are basted together with a crisscross grid of lines of basting.

(Right) The cushion top is quilted along the lines shown in the diagram, by machine or hand.

QUILTING AND PATCHWORK · PROJECT 5

RAINBOW FANS QUILT

Once you have learned how to make one square patchwork block, it's very easy to make several and put them together to make a large quilt.

This rainbow fans quilt is made using the same basic Grandmother's Fan block as the pillow cover project on page 120. Twenty-four of them and one "Dresden Plate" centerpiece are linked with solid-color lattice strips, then surrounded with a simple strip-pieced border to produce a stunning bed cover.

The color pattern for the quilt shown was planned with particular fabrics in mind, but you could assemble the fans from any fabrics. Choose the basic colors that you want to use, and then collect equal amounts of twenty-four solid and printed fabrics in those colors. "Fat quarters" are

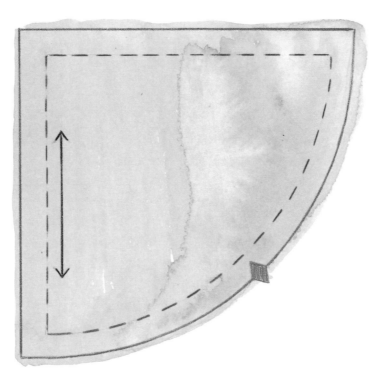

Template A

used. These fabric pieces are generally offered by quilting retailers, who, instead of cutting a strip across the whole width of the material, fold the material in half lengthwise, cut along the fold for ½ yd (0.5 m) and then across to one selvage, yielding a far more useful piece of fabric.

MATERIALS

1 piece of unbleached muslin, or similar neutral background fabric 45 in x 3¼ yd (114 x 325 cm)
24 fat quarters or similar pieces of your chosen fabrics
1 piece of solid-colored fabric 43–44 x 90 in (110–112 x 225 cm)
1 piece of lightweight polyester batting 8–9 sq yd (8–9 sq m)
1 piece of solid backing fabric 7 x 7 ft (2.10 x 2.10 m)
Pink cotton binding strips, 1½ in x 10 yd (4 cm x 9 m)
Matching sewing threads *or*, if quilting by hand, quilting threads
Soft pencil

Preparation

Wash and press all the fabrics you will be using.

Trace the templates onto paper and cut them out of thin cardboard.

From the unbleached muslin cut:
● 25 squares 12½ in (32 cm) square
● 16 squares using template E.

From the solid border fabric cut:
● 4 strips 2½ in (6 cm) wide and 68½ in (174 cm) long (pieces F for the borders)
● 4 strips 3½ in (9 cm) wide and 68½ in (174 cm) long (pieces G for the borders)
● 40 strips 2½ in (6 cm) wide and 12½ in (32 cm) long (pieces H for the

lattice)
● 4 squares 8½ in (21.5 cm) square (pieces I for the border corners).

From your 24 patchwork fabrics cut:
● 1 piece using template A from each fabric (24)
● 6 pieces using template B from each fabric (144)
● 1 piece using template D from each fabric for the Dresden Plate centerpiece (24).

Lay the templates on the wrong side of the fabrics, draw carefully around them with the soft pencil, and cut them out. Mark the seam allowance on the

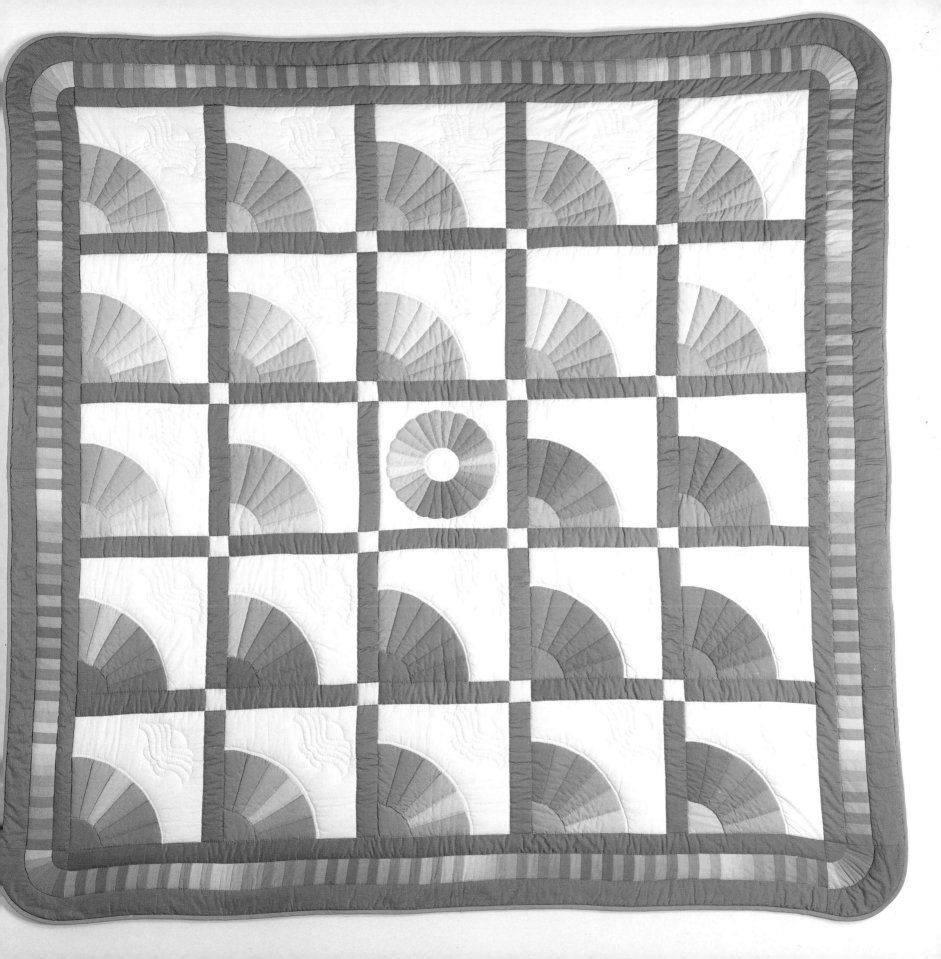

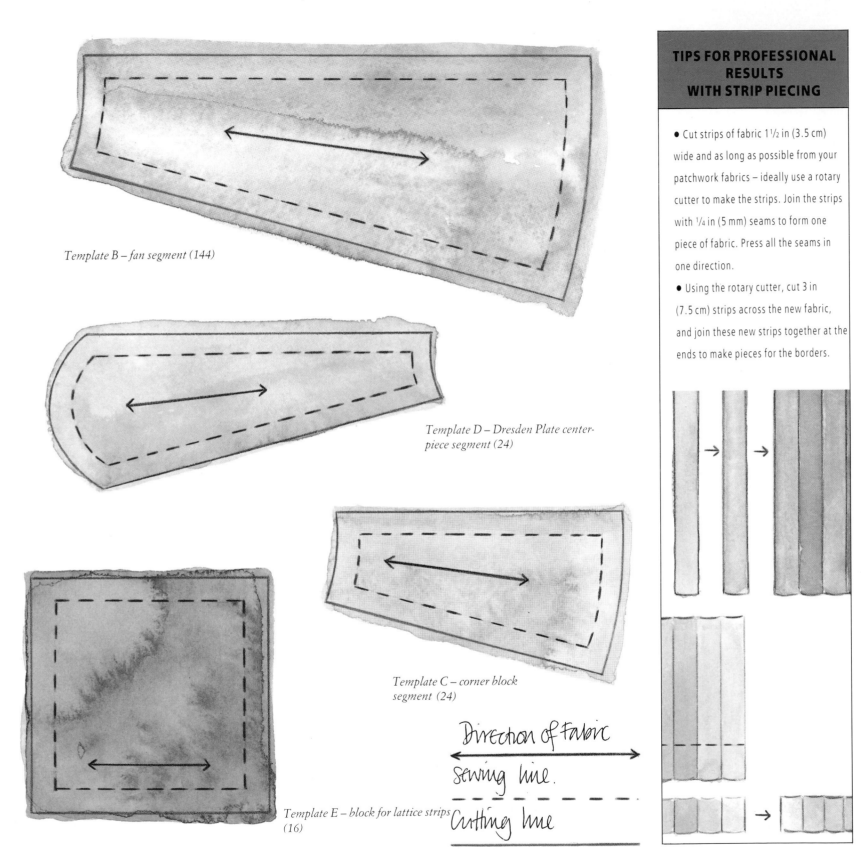

Template B – fan segment (144)

Template D – Dresden Plate center-piece segment (24)

Template C – corner block segment (24)

Template E – block for lattice strips (16)

Direction of Fabric

Sewing line.

Cutting line

TIPS FOR PROFESSIONAL RESULTS WITH STRIP PIECING

● Cut strips of fabric 1½ in (3.5 cm) wide and as long as possible from your patchwork fabrics – ideally use a rotary cutter to make the strips. Join the strips with ¼ in (5 mm) seams to form one piece of fabric. Press all the seams in one direction.

● Using the rotary cutter, cut 3 in (7.5 cm) strips across the new fabric, and join these new strips together at the ends to make pieces for the borders.

Preparation *The templates are drawn around, then cut out.*

The Dresden Plate design for the centerpiece is made using the petal-shaped segments, then applied to the remaining muslin square.

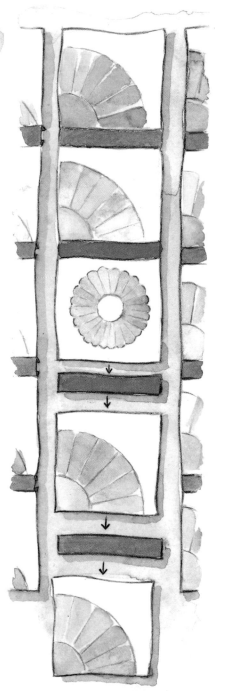

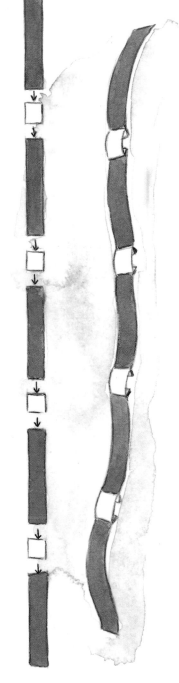

back of each piece.

Then choose any six of your patchwork fabrics – it doesn't matter which ones – and cut four pieces using template C from each of them (24 – these are for the corner blocks). Cut out and mark seam allowances as before.

Using the patchwork pieces, make up 24 Fan blocks as described in the fourth through eighth stages of preparation on page 120.

For the Dresden Plate centerpiece, join all the template D pieces into a circle, pressing all the seams in one direction. Turn under the shaped outside edge and curved inside edge of the patchwork circle, and baste with small stitches, making sure that the curves are smooth, then carefully press it flat.

Stitch the Dresden Plate shape in place in the center of the remaining muslin block using invisible slipstitches; press.

Join the blocks into strips of five separated by four of the H lattice strips. Make sure that the Dresden Plate block is the central block in its strip of five. Press all the seams toward the lattice strips.

Make four long strips, each of five of the H lattice strips and four of your template E shapes. Press all the seams toward the border fabric.

Join the long lattice strips to the block strips, matching the seams carefully.

Press all the seams toward the lattice strips.

Prepare the four corner squares for the border by making small fans as for the blocks but without the inner quarter-circle shape. Use one segment of each fabric in the fans, and appliqué them to the I squares.

Make four border pieces, each 3 x 68½ in (7.5 x 174 cm), by strip-piecing the remainder of the fabrics (see page 126).

For each of the border sides, join one F strip, one strip-pieced border cut to length, and one G strip.

Attach one of these composite strips to the top of the quilt and one to the bottom, with the G strips on the outside.

Stitch a corner block to each end of the remaining two border strips, matching the seams carefully, especially where the strip-piecing joins the corner fans. Press.

Stitch these strips to the sides of the quilt, again matching the seams very carefully, and press flat.

Quilting

1 Place the backing fabric on a flat surface and lay the batting on top. Position the patchwork on top of the batting, and baste the three layers together using lines of crisscross basting.

The blocks are joined in strips of five, with lattice strips between the blocks, with the Dresden Plate block positioned in the center of one of the strips.

Long lattice strips are made by joining rows of short lattice strips separated by muslin squares.

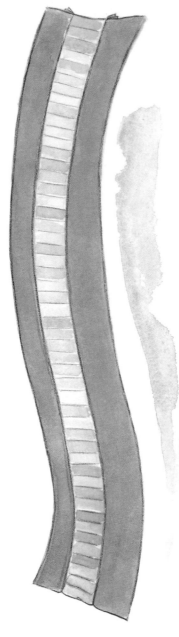

Preparation *The block strips and lattice strips are joined to make the whole patchwork top.*

Tiny fans are made from the small patchwork segments and appliquéd to the border corner blocks.

2 If you are quilting by machine, begin at the center of the quilt, and quilt each seam "in the ditch" (actually stitching along the seamline itself) in machine straight stitch. Stitch in the same way ¼ in (5 mm) outside each fan and the Dresden Plate. Quilt a decorative pattern in the corner of each block. Alternatively, you could use the quilting diagram on the opposite page. For the border, stitch around the strip-pieced section.

If you are quilting by hand, begin in

The borders are made by joining two long strips of border lattice with a strip-pieced length in between them.

- When you are quilting, put a piece of masking tape around the finger you use underneath the quilt to guide the needle back through; this will prevent you from pricking your finger constantly!

- Use a very sharp pencil for marking the seam allowances of your patchwork pieces – the pieces must be very accurate for a good result.

- Put a piece of sandpaper under the fabric pieces when you are marking them; this stops the fabric from moving around.

- Use a rotary cutter and board, if you can, for cutting the strips – this saves a great deal of time in cutting and measuring.

the center of the quilt, and quilt each seam and corner in the same way as for machine quilting, but use short, even running stitches in harmonizing quilting thread.

Finishing

3 Complete the quilt by trimming the edges then binding them (see page 16), rounding the corners to follow the corner fans if you wish.

Variations

If the idea of a double bed quilt seems a bit daunting, make fewer blocks for other smaller projects. For example, try several together in pastel colors for a crib quilt, or join a batch of blocks in bright prints as a "throw" for a sofa, with lattice strips in matching colors. Alternatively, make several squares in upholstery fabrics and join them together to form a rug.

Decorative shape for corner quilting

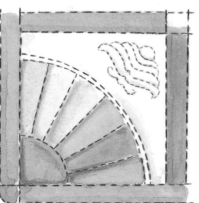

Preparation *Border pieces are added to the top and bottom of the quilt. The corner pieces are joined to the remaining two border pieces, matching the seams carefully, then these borders are stitched to the sides of the patchwork and it is pressed.*

Quilting *Each block is quilted along the seamlines and ¼ in (5 mm) outside the edges of the fans and the Dresden Plate centerpiece.*

INSPIRATION

N ew fabrics, dyes, fabric paints, threads, and sewing machines have opened up myriad possibilities for the humble patchwork quilt. These pages show some traditional and some very modern approaches to the technique.

For this quilt, called Myomi, a commercial pattern was used for the blocks. The pattern was pieced by machine then quilted by hand, filling in the background of each block with a diamond design.

This sawtooth design was produced by stitching strips of patchwork triangles between the alternate stripes of red and white. The quilt was made in the 1880s and is some kind of commemoration – the white stripes are covered with signatures.

Colourwash Stripe III *makes use of many squares of printed cotton, arranged so that they fade from dark to light across the shape. The patchwork has been quilted in a checkered design at an angle to the pieced squares.*

The patchwork quilt below was made around 1910 in England. The central basket motif is appliquéd and the whole design is quilted fairly roughly but cheerfully.

▲ *The traditional hexagon pattern of English patchwork has been transformed in this geometric hanging entitled* Isocomb. *The inspiration for the design came from the quilter's experiments making shaded hexagonal blocks with home-dyed cotton fabrics.*

▶ *The pattern used for this quilt is called* Double Wedding Ring. *It was made as a tenth wedding anniversary present.*
   The pattern is pieced by machine despite all the curved seams, then quilted with different motifs and bound with bias binding.

CHAPTER 9

CORDED QUILTING

Also known as Italian quilting, corded quilting has actually been used in many European countries
for several centuries.
The name "corded" describes it exactly; the relief effect is created not by
stitching layers of fabric together but by inserting cord or yarn in channels that have been stitched through
two layers of fabric. The resulting raised lines cause the design to stand
out against the flat background.
Corded quilting is especially well suited to interwoven patterns such as Celtic designs and knot motifs,
in which the overlapping lines are enhanced by the cords threaded through them.

+   +   +   **CORDED QUILTING · PROJECT 1**   +   +   +

SEWING CADDY

The pretty "pocket" shown here is perfect for holding all your sewing things while you are working. It can also be used as a carry-all if you want to take some sewing away on vacation, for example, but don't want to be burdened with a large workbasket. The stuffed section in the center of the caddy forms a handy pincushion. The design is stitched by hand or by machine in a color slightly darker than the bckground fabric. The design is then threaded using a bodkin carrying tapestry yarn to raise it slightly.

Preparation

Wash and press the fabrics.
Enlarge (see page 26) the pocket pattern and backing pattern to the correct size, and use them as guides to cut the following pieces:
● 2 pocket fronts and 1 backing piece from the mauve cotton
● 1 backing piece from the printed cotton
● 2 pockets from the lining fabric.

Quilting

1 Transfer the design to the fronts of the mauve pocket pieces (see page 12) using the water-soluble or fading pen.
2 Place the lining pieces under the pocket fronts, and baste the two layers firmly together around the design. If you are quilting by machine, use a medium-length straight stitch and the sewing thread to stitch along the lines of the design, finishing the ends off carefully and invisibly.
3 If you are quilting by hand, use four strands of the embroidery floss, and

MATERIALS

1 piece of plain mauve cotton or
  polyester-cotton fabric 18 x 28 in
  (46 x 70 cm)
2 pieces of white or mauve lining fabric
  9 x 11 in (23 x 28 cm)
1 piece of mauve and white patterned
  fabric 9 x 28 in (23 x 70 cm)
1 skein of thick white tapestry yarn
2 skeins of medium purple stranded
  embroidery floss
Small amount of synthetic stuffing
Bodkin
Sewing thread to match the solid
  mauve fabric
Water-soluble *or* fading pen
Small, sharp pair of embroidery
  scissors

Pattern for the pocket front

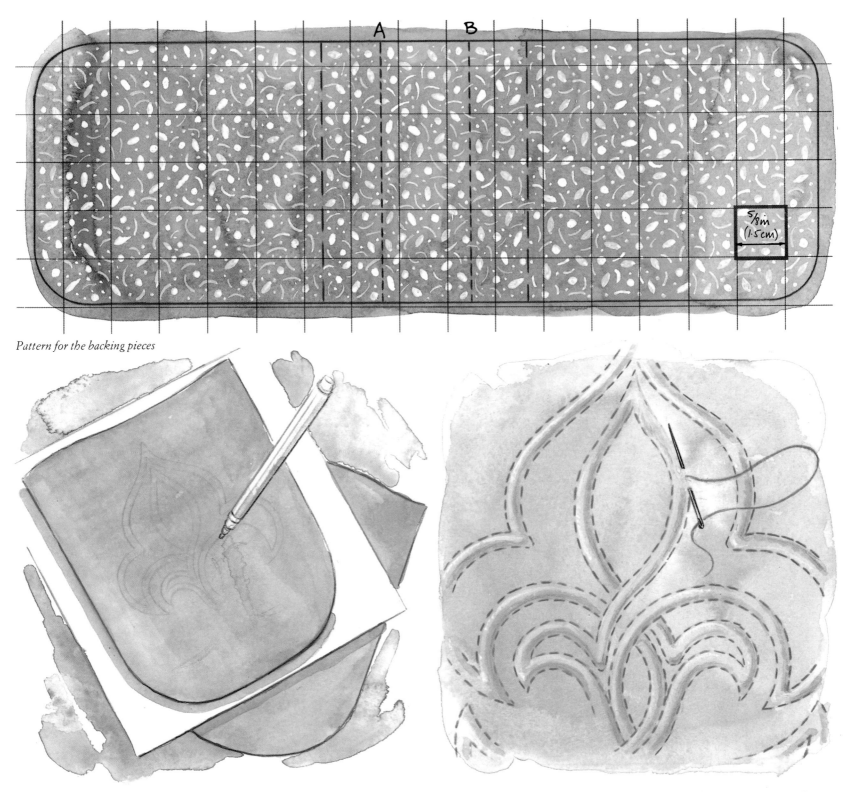

A B

5/8in
(1.5cm)

Pattern for the backing pieces

Quilting. *The design is transferred to the front of each pocket shape.*

The pocket fronts are basted to the pocket linings, then the lines of the design are stitched by machine or by

hand to form the channels for the tapestry yarn.

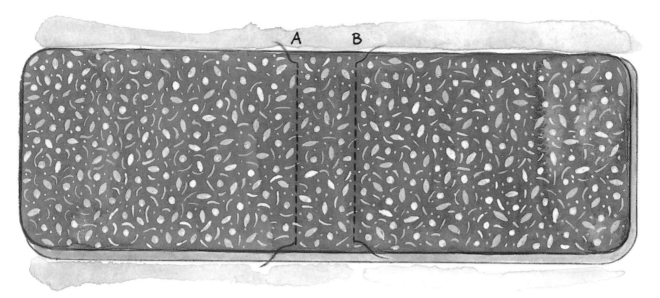

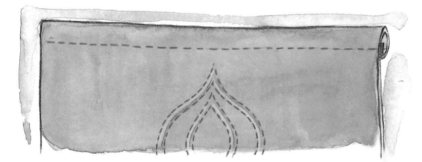

Finishing. The printed backing piece and solid backing piece are stitched together along lines A and B, stopping at the seamline.

A double hem is turned under and stitched along the top edges of the pockets.

stitch along the lines of the design on both pockets with backstitch, taking care to make the stitches even.

4 Remove the basting threads, and sponge away any remaining pen marks.

5 Press the designs gently on the wrong side.

6 Using the sharp embroidery scissors, cut small slits in the backing fabric at the ends of each channel and at every major change of direction.

7 Using three strands of tapestry yarn in the bodkin, thread the yarn through the channels of the design.

8 When the threading is complete, press your work gently on the wrong side.

Finishing

9 Using the water-soluble or fading pen, mark lines on the front of the printed fabric at points A and B. Place the printed fabric on the remaining mauve fabric piece, wrong sides together, and stitch by machine (or backstitch by hand) along the lines, starting and stopping ½ in (1 cm) in from the raw edges.

10 Press under and stitch a small double hem along the top edge of each pocket front.

11 Place the backing piece printed side down, and position the pockets, right

TIPS FOR PROFESSIONAL RESULTS WITH CORDED QUILTING

- Mark the top fabric with your quilting design, preferably using a water-soluble or fading pen, then baste the top fabric to a firm backing fabric.

- Stitch each pair of lines in the design by machine or hand to form a series of channels. If you are stitching by hand, make sure that you produce firm lines of stitching by using backstitch or close running stitches.

- On the back of the fabric, cut small slits – just through the backing fabric – at the ends of each channel and at every major change of direction. Thread the channels with the cord using a bodkin. If you are using very fine cord or just one or two strands of yarn or similar, you can simply make small holes in the fabric using the bodkin, instead of cutting slits. However, at each corner or marked change of direction or at intervals along long lines, bring the needle out and re-insert it, to insure that the thread doesn't pull the pattern out of shape.

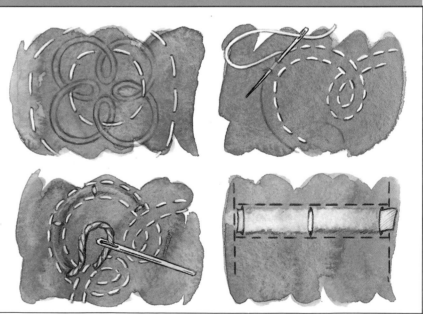

Finishing. *With the right sides of the pockets face down on the back of the printed backing piece, the pocket fronts are stitched to it.*

The pockets are turned right side out, and the gap between stitched lines A and B is stuffed to create a pincushion. Then the raw edges are folded over twice and stitched down to create a plain binding.

TIPS FOR PROFESSIONAL RESULTS

● When you're stuffing the pincushion part, stuff it until it is fairly firm but not rigid: if you put too *little* stuffing in, it won't be thick enough to hold your pins and needles; if you put too *much* in, it will pull the whole caddy out of shape.

● To prevent the pockets from gaping open, attch them to the backing fabric about ½ in (1 cm) in from each edge with a small, invisible stitch.

sides down, at the ends. Pin, baste, and machine stitch a ½ in (1 cm) seam around the curves to the tops of the pockets.

12 Trim the seams, turn the pockets right side out, and press.

13 Fill the channel between the two stitched lines on the printed fabric with stuffing.

14 Fold the raw edges at the sides of the backing piece over twice – folding ¼ in (5 mm) over each time – then pin, baste, and stitch them in place, either by hand or by machine.

Variations

If you don't want your quilting stitches to show so much, you can choose a stranded floss that matches your solid fabric exactly.

For a pretty Victorian effect, make the pockets in a delicate printed fabric, but choose a tiny print, so that the corded shape still shows up and isn't lost in the pattern.

One delicate way of combining corded with shadow quilting is to make the top layer of fabric a sheer organdy or voile and to thread the channels with colored tapestry yarn.

This classic-style motif could also be used to decorate a pocket on a home-tailored shirt or skirt, or even worked in soft leather or suede on a handbag.

CORDED QUILTING · PROJECT 2

$\mathscr{A}$LBUM COVER

For a touch of luxury, this design for a wedding photograph album cover is stitched in white on white silk.

Celtic knot motifs are often designed so that the pattern is formed of one continuous line, interweaving numerous times, to symbolize eternity, but this design uses *two* interwoven lines to symbolize two lives woven together.

The size and shape of the design fits a standard wedding photograph album, but could easily be adapted to suit albums of other sizes and shapes.

You don't need an extra lining for the quilting, since the slits cut in the back are concealed by the album itself.

Preparation

Trace the chart for the album cover onto thick paper or thin card.
Press the fabrics.

Quilting

1 Using the water-soluble or fading pen, transfer the design (see page 12) onto the right-hand edge of the piece of silk, positioning it so that the right-hand edge of the design is 4 in (10 cm) in from the edge of the fabric and there are even-sized borders of fabric above and below the design.
2 Place the marked silk right side up over the backing fabric, and baste the two layers together securely around the edge of the design and across the middle.

MATERIALS
1 white photograph album 11 x 12 in (28 x 31 cm)
1 piece of white or ivory slubbed silk fabric approximately 16 x 30 in (42 x 75 cm)
1 piece of white backing fabric the same size as the silk fabric
1 skein of white or ivory stranded cotton *or* silk embroidery floss
Fine filler cord 5 yd (4.5 m) long
All-purpose glue
Large bodkin
White paper slightly smaller than the front and back covers of the album
Water-soluble *or* fading pen
Small, sharp embroidery scissors

Quilting *The design is marked on the white silk at the right-hand edge, then the silk and backing fabric are basted together around the design and across the middle.*

Quilting *The design is stitched by hand, then the basting threads and any remaining pen marks are removed. The channels are quilted with the fine filler cord.*

Design for the album cover

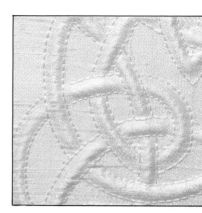

Finishing *The quilted fabric is laid face down on a flat surface and the photo album laid open on top of it. The edges*

of the fabric are trimmed and clipped evenly round the edges of the album as shown.

colored silk or stitched on organdy and quilted with colored cord. The design would also look stunning stitched as stained glass appliqué in vibrant colors (see page 102).

If you want to make a wedding album cover, but you're a little wary of working with white silk, choose a silk fabric that picks up another color from the wedding – for example, the color of the flowers or the bridesmaids' dresses.

Many other Celtic designs can be adapted for Italian quilting; look through books in your local library for inspiration.

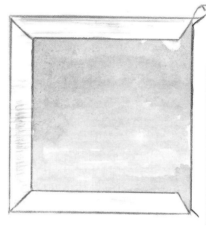

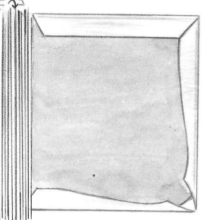

The clipped edges are glued down over the inside front and inside back of the album cover, using the all-purpose glue;

the fabric is stretched taut as it is glued down.

3 Using three strands of the stranded cotton or silk floss, backstitch along all the lines of the design, taking care to make the stitches even.

4 Remove the basting, and wipe away any remaining soluble pen lines with a damp cloth.

5 Press the design gently on the back.

6 Using very sharp embroidery scissors, cut slits in the backing cloth at the ends of the channels and at any corners, then thread the filler cord through using the bodkin (see page 136).

7 If necessary, press the embroidery gently on the back.

Finishing

8 Lay the quilted fabric right side down on a flat surface, and open the photograph album on top of it. Carefully cut away the sections of fabric shown in the diagram, and trim the rest so that it is about 1¼ in (3 cm) larger than the album all around.

9 Fold the edges over the album front and back and glue them down with the all-purpose glue.

10 Trim the two pieces of white paper, if necessary, and glue these over the raw edges inside the album covers (if the album endpapers are suitable, you could use them to cover the raw edges instead).

11 Lightly glue the two sections of fabric at the top and bottom of the spine, if necessary, then tuck them down between the spine binding and the edges of the pages.

Variations

This Celtic knot design is very versatile – try it on a pillow cover in solid, richly

● It is important to choose a white album for your base, for even though the front and back will be covered, a dark album might show through the pale fabric.

● When you're laying out the fabric to trim the edges in stage 8, make sure that you have got the album opened fully flat on top *before* you do so; otherwise it may appear smaller than it really is.

● Don't be tempted to glue the back of the quilted area to the front of the album, as the glue might seep through the fabric and spoil its appearance. You should be able to make the design lie fully flat by stretching it as you glue it down around the edges.

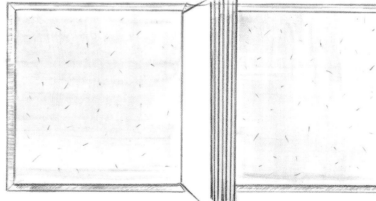

The insides of the album cover are finished by glueing paper over the raw edges, and the tabs of fabric left at the

top and bottom of the spine are tucked down between the spine binding and the page edges.

CORDED QUILTING · PROJECT 3

CHINESE HEADBOARD

This project shows how adaptable corded quilting can be. The basic technique is the same as for the previous projects, but has been scaled up and used for a very large design. For this striking geometric pattern, based on a traditional Chinese screen design, the channels for the cord are formed by stitching colored woven tape onto a plain white background. Obviously larger channels need larger cord, so this design makes use of thin synthetic rope. Once the quilting is complete, the design is mounted onto a foam pad to form a comfortable cushion.

MATERIALS

2 pieces of strong white fabric 24 x 56 in (60 x 142 cm), 2 pieces 4 x 24 in (10 x 60 cm), and 2 pieces 4 x 56 in (10 x 142 cm)

4 strips of blue fabric 10 x 12 in (25 x 30 cm)

Blue seam binding or similar tape 1 in (2.5 cm) wide and 18 yd (15 m) long

Blue and white sewing thread

Synthetic rope about 3/8 in (8 mm) in diameter and 18 yd (16 m) long

1 foam pad 2 in (5 cm) thick measuring 22 x 54 in (55 x 137 cm)

Roll of wallpaper *or* shelf-lining paper for enlarging the chart

Black felt-tip pen

Water-soluble or fading pen

Preparation

Wash and press the fabrics.

Enlarge (see page 26) the design to the correct size and mark the lines with the black felt-tip pen.

Put one of the large pieces of the white fabric over the chart, and trace the lines of the design showing through with the water-soluble or fading pen.

Quilting

1 Lay the marked fabric on a flat surface, and pin the blue tape along the lines of the design, cutting it where lines cross. Pleat the tape carefully where it has to turn corners to miter them; where the tape begins and ends on each part of the design, fold the ends under diagonally so that they look like the other corners. Where one line runs into another, cut the lower tape slightly longer so that it tucks under the upper tape and will be secured by the top tape's stitching.

2 When all the tapes have been pinned in place, baste them to the backing

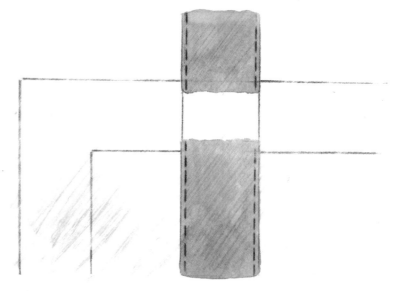

Preparation The design is marked on the right side of the headboard front; make sure that the lines are straight and the corners square.

Quilting The tape is basted firmly in position along the marked lines, and where one line overlaps another, the underneath tapes are positioned as shown. The tape is pleated where it turns corners or folded under on the diagonal where it joins a new tape at a corner.

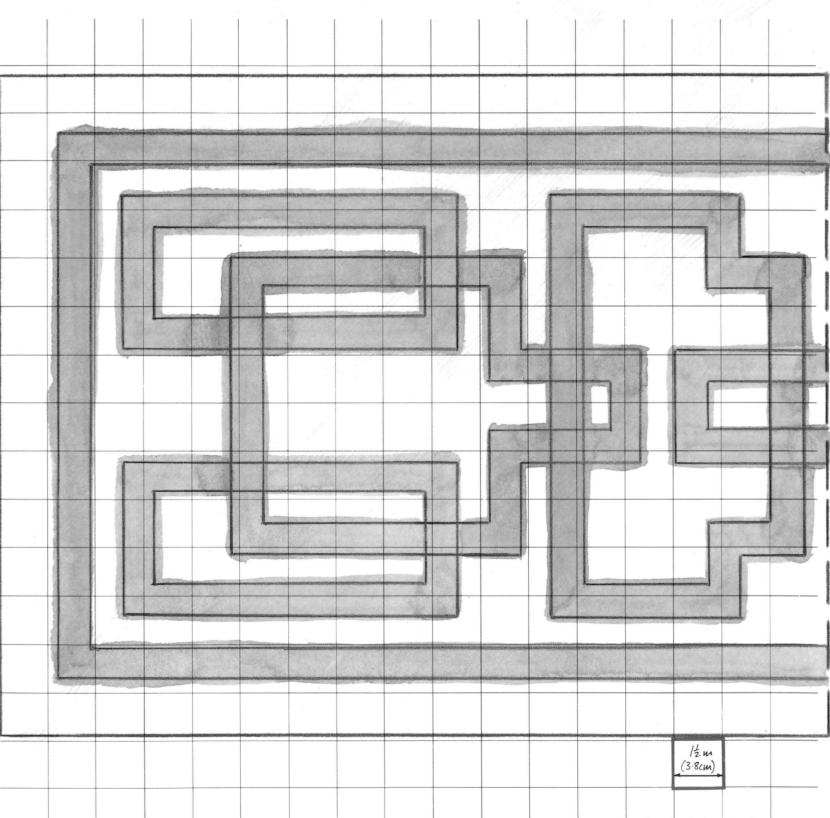

1½ in
(3.8cm)

Chart for the headboard

Quilting *The tapes are stitched in position along both edges, and the corner folds are slipstitched in place,* *through the tape only, not through the background fabric.*

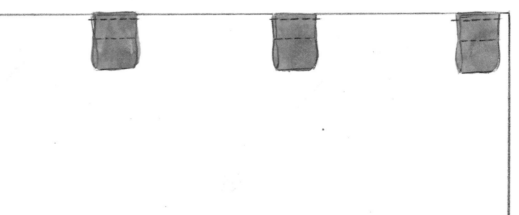

Photographic detail shows tapes stitched into position.

Finishing *The blue fabric strips are seamed and topstitched. They are then* *folded into loops and sewn to the right side of the cushion back at even* *intervals along the top, as shown.*

fabric for extra security.

3 Using the blue thread, machine stitch along both edges of each tape. Don't stitch down the diagonal folds on the corners; just stitch down the edges.

4 Secure the corner folds with blue slipstitches worked by hand, making sure that you stitch only through the *tape*, not into the backing fabric.

5 Following the instructions on page 136, thread each channel with the synthetic rope (the rope should be firm enough for you to just push it through each channel, as you will not be able to use any kind of bodkin).

Finishing

6 With right sides together, stitch a 1 in (2.5 cm) seam along the long edges of each of the blue fabric strips. Turn them right side out and press. Topstitch in white along both edges of the strips.

7 Fold the strips in half, aligning the raw ends, and topstitch across their width about halfway down (this makes a casing for the curtain rod to slip through). Pin the loops in position on the top front edge of the cushion back, and machine stitch across them, close to

TIPS FOR PROFESSIONAL RESULTS

• If you cut a length of thin cardboard the exact width of your tape, you can use this to measure and mark the lines as you trace them onto the white fabric, which will mean that your lines will be straighter than if you trace them all

freehand. Some yardsticks are exactly 1 in (2.5 cm) wide, so they can be used in the same way.

• Use straight seam binding instead of bias binding for this design, as bias

binding will stretch, and you want the tapes to stay as firm as possible.

Finishing The edge pieces are joined to form a continuous strip, and this is basted to the quilted cushion front, matching the corners carefully with the right sides together. The seam is then stitched by machine.

The edge pieces are basted to the cushion back along three sides, then machine stitched together, with the fourth side left open so that the cover can be turned right side out.

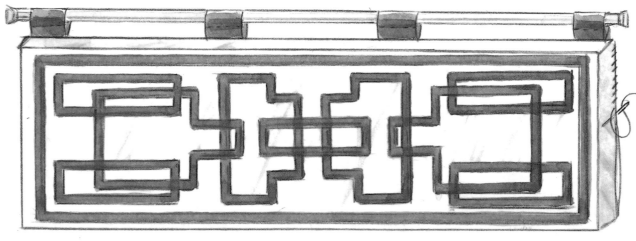

The cushion cover is stuffed with the foam pad and the open edges are then closed with slipstitches; or a zipper is inserted so that the cover can be removed for cleaning.

the raw edges of the cushion back fabric, several times.

8 With the right sides together, stitch the four remaining pieces of white fabric together across their widths in 1 in (2.5 cm) seams.

9 With right sides together, pin, baste, and machine stitch this ring of fabric to the quilted front, matching the seams in the side fabrics to the corners of the front piece, in 1 in (2.5 cm) seam ; press the seam open.

10 With right sides together, pin, baste, and machine stitch the side pieces to the cushion back in a 1 in (2.5 cm) seam, leaving one side open. Press the seam open, and turn the cover right side out.

11 Insert the foam pad through the opening, and either slipstitch the sides of the opening together or turn the raw edges under and insert a zipper.

12 Hang the cushion from a blue or natural wood curtain rod mounted on the wall at the head of the bed so that the cushion hangs at a comfortable height.

Variations

Any color of fabric and tape can be used for the headboard design. For a subtle effect, use two shades of one color, or appliqué a plain tape to a softly patterned background.

For a double bed, extend some of the horizontal lines of the pattern, but work out the design on a piece of paper before you transfer it to the fabric.

Threaded tape designs have a variety of uses – try personalizing a child's sports bag by stitching on initials in tape and then threading them with thick cord, for example. You can use the same technique to provide color and texture where you don't want bulk – for example, on a garment. A geometrical threaded tape design can look striking as a border on a skirt, around a collar and cuffs, or down the sleeves of a blouse.

Jackets with threaded tape designs look very dramatic. Lay out your pattern pieces and decide which areas you want to decorate with the design, then work out your design on paper so that it fits the shapes of the paper pattern. Cut out your fabric pieces and stitch the tapes to them. Generally you'll find this easier to do before you have stitched any seams, though if your pattern needs to cross any seams, such as around the jacket hem, you may need to stitch all or some of the tapes on after the basic shape has been stitched. Then thread the tapes through before you attach the lining, so that the lining covers the slits that you have cut.

If you have made the headboard, you may like to add some other threaded tape patterns in other parts of your bedroom decor to echo the headboard design. Try making a border at the bottom or down the center seam of plain curtains – perhaps using narrower tape and cord in a reduced-size version of the blue-and-white design or one of the alternatives on this page. Or, if you're feeling really creative, you could embroider a rug in large crossstitch on rug canvas, or pick up the design across the top of a comforter cover or bedspread. For a fully coordinated look, you might like to try fabric-painting the design on the top edge of a sheet, or making it into a repeat pattern to be stenciled around the walls as a frieze.

TIPS FOR PROFESSIONAL RESULTS

● If you use nylon rope for threading the tapes, you obviously won't be able to thead it onto any kind of bodkin. To stop the ends fraying carefully hold them in a flame for a few seconds. This will bond them and give the rope a harder tip which will be easier to push through the tapes.

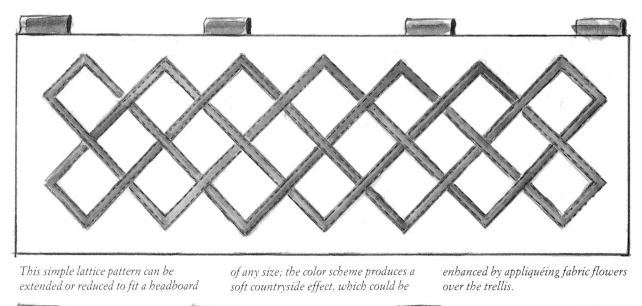

This simple lattice pattern can be extended or reduced to fit a headboard *of any size; the color scheme produces a soft countryside effect, which could be* *enhanced by appliquéing fabric flowers over the trellis.*

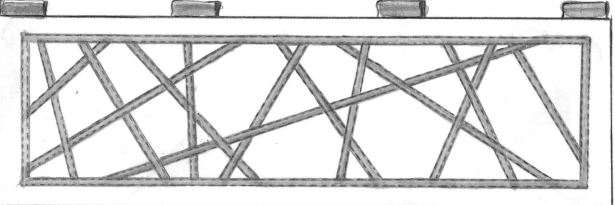

This pretty green-on-green design uses random straight lines *interweaving across the shape of the headboard; you don't have to use the* *arrangement shown here – you can adapt it to the exact dimensions.*

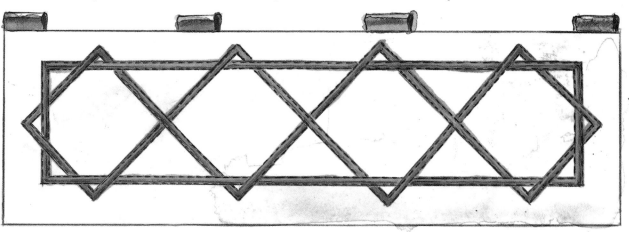

This stark variation on the trellis pattern looks very high-tech: use *it as part of a simple color scheme such as black, white, gray, and red, or for a* *bold look use a combination of bright primary colors.*

INSPIRATION

Corded quilting is an ancient technique, but it has lost none of its appeal; today's quilters are still producing beautiful corded work and also experimenting with new effects.

▼ *In this piece, lengths of tubing have been made of bright fabric and then threaded with several strands of thick yarn to pad them. The tubes have been woven into an intricate octagon and stitched around where they overlap at the edges of the shape.*

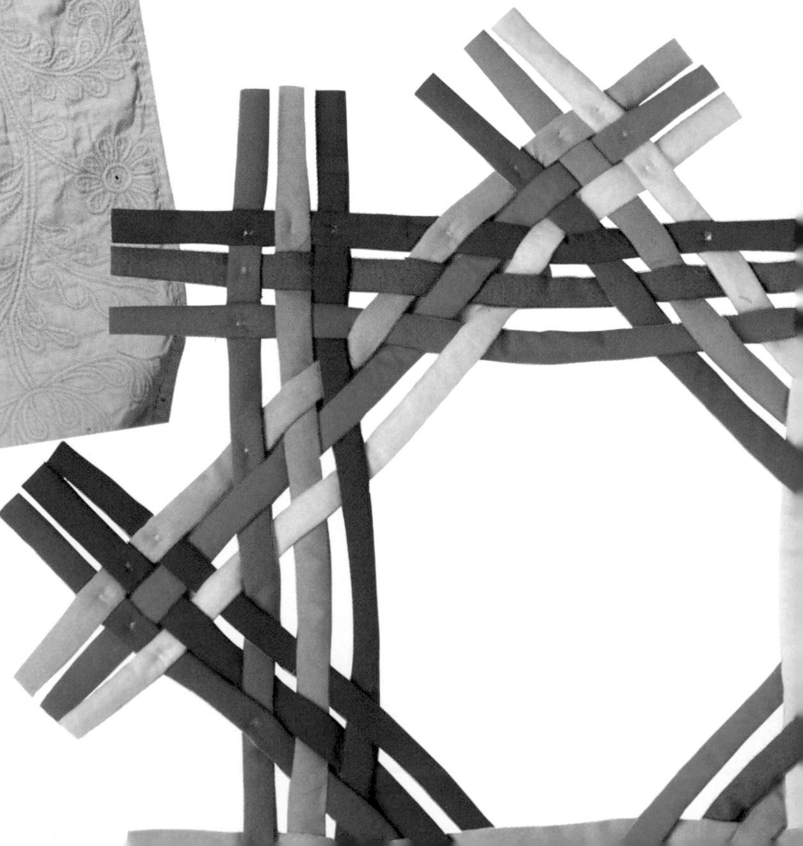

The corded quilt shown here is worked in an ornate pattern; it was made in the 18th century. Tiny white backstitches have been stitched on white linen to make the channels for the cords.

▼ In this panel the potential of corded quilting for gathering fabric has been exploited. Rectangles of different sizes were cut from different colored fabrics with pinking shears, and appliquéd to the background with channels of machine stitching. Thick cord was inserted into the channels at the back and pulled up tightly, then the outside of the background fabric was gathered into a black binding.

The pieces of corded quilting above were done to experiment with the technique. On the left-hand side the stitched channels have been corded from the back; on the other side they have been corded from the front, and the ends of the cords have then been fluffed out.

▼ Striped fabrics are ideal for corded quilting, as they provide the stitching guides. In the cushion below, the purple stripes have been stitched on each side to provide channels, which have been threaded with thin filler cord, allowing the fabric to gather slightly to give a pretty texture.

CHAPTER 10

SASHIKO QUILTING

Sashiko (pronounced "sash-ko") quilting is an ancient Japanese technique. Several thin layers of fabric are stitched together with running stitches in geometric patterns. Sometimes many different stitch patterns are used in one item, sometimes just one; but the stitching is worked so that the threads themselves form the main pattern – they are not there just to provide texture. So, whereas in basic quilting the running stitches are often worked as unobtrusively as possible, in Sashiko quilting they are larger and often worked in a contrasting thread, each stitch twice as long on the front of the fabric as it is on the back. Sashiko quilting is sometimes padded with a thin layer of batting, but it can be worked with flat fabrics, too.

+ + + **SASHIKO QUILTING · PROJECT 1** + + +

TABLE TOP CLOTH

The exotic print chosen for the background of this table top cloth and the elaborate braid used around the edge enhance the Oriental look produced by the wavy lines of quilting. We've used white matte embroidery cotton to give a good firm texture to the embroidery, but stranded floss, pearl cotton, or thick silk threads would look equally attractive. Cut the fabric to fit your own tray, then work out how many repeat patterns you can fit into the area.

Preparation
Wash and press the fabrics.
Trace the stitching design onto a piece of paper (see page 12).

Quilting
1 Fold the printed fabric in half, then in quarters, creasing the folds slightly with your thumbnail, then unfold. Using the dressmaker's carbon paper, transfer the design to the right side of the fabric (see page 12), working outward in even blocks from the center point so that the design is centered on the fabric. Stop when you have drawn the last complete repeat of the shape within about 2 in (5 cm) of each of the edges.
2 Draw a straight line along the edges of the last repeats.
3 Lay the white backing fabric right side down on a flat surface, and place the printed fabric right side up on top. Baste the two layers together around the edges and across the fabric in a couple of places.
4 Using the matte cotton, work running stitch neatly along the pattern lines and the straight border. Make the stitches twice as long on the front as they are on the back.

MATERIALS
1 piece of green printed cotton fabric 18 x 24 in (45 x 60 cm)
1 piece of white cotton backing fabric the same size as the printed fabric
2 skeins of white matte embroidery cotton
Thick white braid 2 yd (2 m) long
White sewing thread
Pale dressmaker's carbon paper

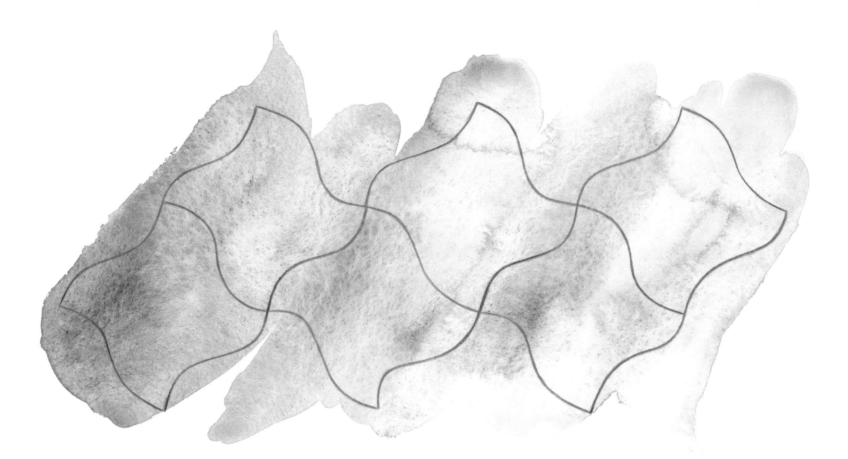

TIPS FOR PROFESSIONAL RESULTS

• If you are using a dark, printed fabric like the one used here, ordinary water-soluble and fading pens won't show up properly, so either use pale dressmaker's carbon paper as directed or draw the design on in light washable crayon or sharp tailor's chalk pencil.

• If you want to reduce bulk around the hem, turn it under just once and stitch it down with medium-length zigzag machine stitching or, if your sewing machine has it, hemming stitch.

• Use a large, sharp needle for working the quilting, as you will need to make quite a large hole in the closely woven fabric in order to pull the cotton through.

Chart for the quilting design

5 When the stitching is complete, remove the basting threads.

Finishing
6 Press a small double hem under to the back all around the table top cloth, and stitch it down by machine or hem it in place by hand.
7 Stitch the white braid along the stitching line on the right side all around the hem of the mat by machine or hand.

Variations
Adapt the design of the table top cloth to make different shapes according to your needs – to fit on a dressing table, say, or a circular coffee table. Just draw in the number of repeats that will fit within the shape, then draw the border

around the edge. Make the table top cloths using one of the other stitch patterns shown on page 173.

Sashiko quilting is very good for garments, as you don't need bulky batting, so liven up a plain jacket or coat by quilting sections with geometric designs.

Quilting *The design is marked onto the front of the printed fabric, then it is*   *tacked firmly to the backing fabric.*

The lines of the design are stitched along in neat running stitches that are   *twice as long on the front of the fabric as they are on the back.*

Finishing *A double hem is turned under along all the raw edges and*   *stitched down by hand or machine to the back of the mat.*

The white braid is positioned round the edges of the right side of the mat and   *stitched into place by machine or hand.*

SASHIKO QUILTING · PROJECT 2

$\mathcal{S}$PRING WALLHANGING

The beautiful abstract shape of this quilting is based on the Chinese character for spring, and the subject is reflected in the soft colors used. The piece of silk used for the background is dyed with gentle blends of pinks, mauves, and blues, and then threads in the same color ranges are used for the stitching.

The pattern is a simple repeat of equilateral triangles, which are stitched in straight lines across the shape in three directions, and the design is completed with a line of quilting around the edge.

Tassels are made from a selection of the threads and stitched to the design at intervals.

Preparation

Press the fabrics.

Enlarge (see page 26) the chart to the correct size onto a large piece of paper.

MATERIALS

1 piece of white silk 40 in (1 m) square
1 piece of white backing fabric the same size as the silk fabric
A selection of threads in pinks, blues, purples, and mauves (use any mixture of stranded floss, ordinary sewing threads, pearl cotton, matte embroidery cotton, threads of different thicknesses, silks, etc.)
Silk paints in pink and blue
Two lengths of bamboo or dowel to fit the top and bottom of the finished hanging
Water-soluble *or* fading pen

In a selection of paper cups, mix up several dilute colors in the pink, blue, and mauve range (make mauves by mixing some pink and blue in different amounts).

Lay sheets of plain paper on a flat surface, and lay the silk on top. Wet the fabric thoroughly by spraying it with water.

Using a wide brush, paint the dilute silk paints onto the fabric; where two colors meet, brush that area with extra water to make the shades run into each other. Leave the edges of the fabric unpainted, fading the colors out gently as you move toward the edges.

Leave the silk to dry completely.

Lay the silk out on a flat surface, right side up, and transfer the spring design to it using water-soluble or fading pen.

Using the same pen, draw a series of parallel lines straight across the shape, from side to side, with exactly 1 in (2.5 cm) gaps between each line. Draw the lines only within the outlines of the spring design.

Choose any point along one of these lines near the center of the shape, and draw a diagonal line at 60° from the horizontal. Draw another series of lines parallel to this one, again making them exactly 1 in (2.5 cm) apart.

You should now be able to join up the intersections on the lines with a third series of parallel lines at the opposite angle, to produce a grid of equilateral triangles.

Quilting

1 Lay the backing fabric right side down on a flat surface, and position the silk on top, right side up. Baste the two layers together with lines of basting stitches around the outside of the marked shape.

1½ in
(3.8cm)

Chart for spring design

Preparation *A series of parallel lines is drawn at even intervals across the* *spring design using the water-soluble or fading pen.*

Another series of parallel lines is drawn at 60° to the first ones, making sure *that they are spaced evenly.*

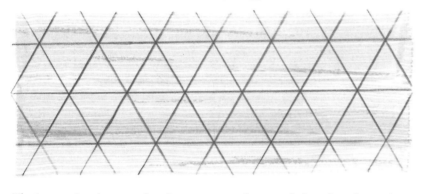

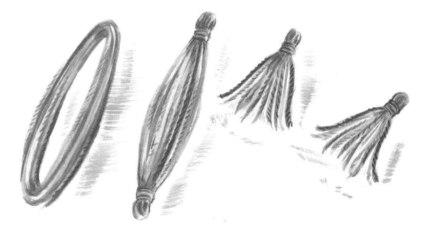

The intersections between these lines are joined with diagonal lines to *produce a grid of equilateral triangles.*

Finishing Loops of mixed threads are bound at the top and bottom, then cut across the middle to produce two tassels to decorate the edges of the design.

(see page 44)

TIPS FOR PROFESSIONAL RESULTS

• If you don't feel confident about painting your silk, work the design on a solid color, or choose an iridescent silk, which incorporates different shades.

• Put lots of variety and texture into the stitching by using two different threads in the needle at once – for example, two colors of stranded floss or a pale matte cotton with a strand of darker silk, or a matte thread together with a strand of metallic thread.

2 Using the various threads, stitch along the straight lines and the outline of the shape, using running stitches and making the stitches on the top of the fabric twice as long as the stitches on the back.

Finishing

3 Make small tassels by winding loops of mixed threads around several fingers. Slip the loops off, and wind thread around a short way in from the top and bottom. Cut the loops across the center, to produce two tassels. Make several more, and sew them on at different points around the edges of the design.
4 Fold under a double hem to the wrong side at each side of the wall-hanging, and stitch it down by machine or by hand.
5 Fold under a small turning to the wrong side at the top and bottom of the

hanging, then fold under again by about 1½ in (4 cm) and stitch along the edge of the first fold to make casings for the bamboo or dowel.
6 Sew two fabric loops or curtain rings, or work buttonhole stitch loops, on the back of the casing where they are hidden from view; use these to hang up the embroidery. Alternatively, make a cord by twisting together some of the threads you have used for quilting and attach it to each end of the top rod.

Variations

Find other Oriental characters meaning different things – for example, happiness, peace, home, or the other seasons –and work them in Sashiko quilting, choosing appropriate paint and thread colors.

This design also works scaled down for a pillow or the back of a housecoat.

You can use the Sashiko quilting technique or a mixture of contrasting fabrics as in shadow quilting (see page 44).

If you want to test your skills, choose a more complex stitching pattern from the examples on page 173, and work that in the shape instead of the triangles. Or divide your shape into several different sections and work each section in a different Sashiko pattern, perhaps with each section stitched in a different color.

You could choose the outline of a Bonsai tree or origami shape. A book on Chinese brush painting or Oriental design will give you further inspiration.

*I*NSPIRATION

Although Sashiko is quite a simple technique, the results it produces can be spectacular, as you can see from the contemporary Sashiko work on these pages. Intense color schemes seem to suit the opulence of the Japanese designs, with blue being an obvious favorite.

The pair of cuffs shown left have been stitched on gold silk using the wineglass pattern of overlapping circles; the cuffs are lightly padded for extra texture.

▼ *The wineglass pattern has also been used on this pillow cover. The circles have been carefully drawn onto the background fabric so that an even border of solid fabric is left around them at the edges of the cushion, then the lines have been stitched in white Sashiko quilting.*

This wallhanging has been divided into quarters diagonally, and each quarter has been stitched in a different geometric pattern. The strong diagonals are broken up by different Oriental motifs, each one basically circular, stitched in the same color scheme of white on blue.

This beautiful jacket
has been made to
a simple pattern
to show off the
irregular areas
of Sashiko
quilting.
Each
section
of stitching on
the front and
back of the jacket
uses a different geometric
pattern, and the quilting has
been done so that the stitching shows as
a neat pattern on the lining.

▶ Several Sashiko patterns overlap on
this wall-hanging. A large flower forms
a central medallion, and a border of
smaller flowers acts as a transition
between two contrasting background
textures, stars, and clamshells. Little
fan shapes complete the corners.

▲ Sashiko quilting has been used to
produce stitched detail on these two
bags. The bag on the left has made use
of one self-contained motif, the fan, and
the other uses a section of a geometric
design. At the edges each design has
been stitched around with a double row
of quilting for extra emphasis.

▶ Blues in the Night makes use of an
interweaving hexagon pattern for the
Sashiko quilting, echoing the hexagon
pieces of fabric used for making the
basic patchwork. The prints of the
fabrics chosen help to emphasize the
idea of a starry night.

DESIGNING YOUR OWN QUILT

Designing your own quilt is easy. As with any other skill, all you need to do is follow a series of basic steps to help you get your ideas out of your head and onto the fabric. Making trial pieces, rather than launching straight into a full-size design, is often a good idea; and flexibility is the key — you may find that your original design concept grows and changes as you work on it.

DESIGNING YOUR OWN QUILT

If you have worked through some of the projects in this book, and experimented with different quilting skills, you may well be at the stage where you would like to design your own quilted project, using your own quilting pattern. Where do you start?

If you follow a few very simple steps in developing your ideas, you'll find that you can easily work out the kind of design you want and then work through sensible ways of applying it to your chosen item. Developing your ideas step by step will prevent you from getting bogged down with unformed ideas.

SOURCES OF INSPIRATION

Once you're familiar with the basic techniques of quilting, you'll soon begin to see the seeds of quilting designs in almost everything around you! Architecture, carpet patterns, wrought iron work, patterns of light on water, drapery fabrics – virtually any decorative shape can be worked up into a quilting pattern of some kind.

In these pages we look at the development of three very different quilting designs from the same inspirational source. You can apply the same process of developing a design to any pattern that you think might have possibilities.

The inspiration

The basic inspiration for the designs was a photograph of an ancient Egyptian stone column. The main pattern up the length of the column is an elongated variation of what quilters know as clam shell – a pattern that is found in the artefacts of many ancient civilizations. Each long clam shell is edged with a thick border, which immediately conjures up images of channels for corded quilting.

The rough ideas

First of all, take a large sheet of paper – or several sheets – and just sketch away very roughly, allowing the shapes themselves to suggest patterns and combinations to you. Don't try to make the designs neat at this stage, as this will interrupt the flow of your thoughts. Put shapes together, turn them around at angles, do mirror images, use them in different sizes, overlap them, and so on (the drawings here show this process at work). Scribble notes alongside your rough designs as you get different ideas for textures, fabrics, techniques, colors, and so on.

Selecting design ideas

By this stage, you will be beginning to get a feel for which combinations and patterns you think will work best. Try these ideas out on fresh sheets of paper a little more neatly to see how they look in isolation and how you might use them

for your quilting project.

It may be that the shape itself will suggest a particular quilted item to you. Think through which quilting technique or techniques will be most suitable and what threads and colors you feel would work best.

Finished design

Draw your design neatly to the required size (using the method described on page 26 if necessary). At this stage, measure lines and curves carefully and make sure that all the shapes of the pattern are consistent.

Try out different fabrics and threads against the pattern, to see what works best. You may want to work a small trial piece in your chosen materials to check that the texture and balance are right.

Once you are completely happy, transfer the design to your chosen fabric (see page 12) and start quilting!

Preliminary sketches experimenting with varied interpretations and arrangements of the elongated clamshell.

Swatches of fabrics and threads can be tried together to see how well they relate. Color cards for paints or fabrics are often useful for expanding your ideas.

The final design and finished piece of stitching, worked in Sashiko quilting in silver thread on a background of red satin.

WORKING THROUGH A DESIGN

Every time you have an idea for a quilting project, jot it down somewhere, otherwise you'll forget it. You may find it helpful to keep a special notebook or file specifically for this purpose. You don't need to draw it neatly; just make a quick sketch or scribble down written ideas, such as "Try something based on the patterns of Indian rugs." Then, when you're feeling in a creative mood, you can pull out your ideas and select which ones you wish to work up into finished designs.

Here you can see how I worked through the design process for a quilt – right from the very first scribbles of inspiration to the finished piece.

The first idea

When I go away on vacation I take a notebook with me for writing down quilting and embroidery ideas; but most of the time I scribble them on the back of old photocopies and put them in a file alongside interesting photo-

graphs, cards, and textures torn from magazines and brochures. This quilt began as one of those scribbles.

I am utterly uninterested in the game of chess, but I have always been fascinated by the shapes of chess pieces and the wonderful contrasts offered by the constantly changing arrangements of black and white as the pieces move across the board. It suddenly occurred to me one evening what a striking design it would make to overlap outlines of chess pieces of different sizes, building in a counterchange of black and white. When I tried to draw even a rough scribble I realized how ignorant I was of just what the pieces looked like, so I

made a note to myself to research the different shapes.

Working out the shapes

I went to the library and looked at books about playing chess and about collecting chess sets. I took photocopies of many interesting sets for later reference.

Deciding on the design elements

Reluctantly I had to abandon less conventional shapes, including some of the more abstract modern ones, as I felt it was important for the shapes to be instantly recognizable as chess pieces. These line drawings show the final shapes I decided on for the pieces; they

are a hybrid of several standard chess set designs.

The design itself

I wanted the quilt to be square – to echo the shape of the chessboard itself – so I drew a large square on paper and began roughing in the shapes in different sizes, rubbing out and re-drawing as the design took shape.

My aim was to end up with a good contrast of sizes among the shapes, as I felt that otherwise they would tend to blur into each other. I also wanted to introduce several random areas of checkering to emphasize the chess theme and to provide visual interest. First of all I made these of varying-sized squares, as I had done with the pieces themselves, but this proved too distracting, so I changed them so that the checkers were all the same size. The drawing shows the final design I came up with, shaded roughly to indicate the areas of black and white.

The quilt itself

I enlarged the design in sections on an enlarging photocopier, because I liked the flow of the lines I had come up with and didn't want to lose them by enlarging the design freehand.

When I had traced the design onto fabric, I painted it in with black fabric paint. I considered appliquéing the black areas, but I wanted to quilt them with a thin line of machine stitching around the shapes, so felt that it was better not to have raw edges.

I layered the finished design with fairly thick batting and white backing fabric, then bound the edges with the backing fabric to complete it. It's come a long way since that first experimental scribble....

Above *The final design for the chess quilt, incorporating the chessmen in different sizes.*

Right *The finished quilt – a dramatic study in black-and-white.*

DESIGNING BY SEWING MACHINE

All of the machine-quilted projects in this book can be stitched on any sewing machine that does straight stitch and zigzag, but these days more and more new machines come with built-in "automatic" stitches – patterns that you can program the machine to repeat down the stitching line. These patterns vary from the simple to the complex, but even the simple ones open up whole new vistas for the quilter.

Fabrics for machine quilting

Natural fibers such as cotton and silk are best and most amenable to quilting by machine. It is possible to use some polyester and mixed-fiber fabrics, but you need to experiment. Generally you need light- to medium-weight fabrics for good results.

For the top layer, choose a closely-woven solid-color fabric for fancy quilting. Stripes, plaids, and patterned fabrics may suggest ideas for patterns, but make sure that the stitches complement the print rather than fight it.

For the batting, you will find medium- to high-loft polyester is about right.

For the bottom layer choose a fabric similar to the top layer if you are not going to stitch in a lining, or use light-weight cotton, such as muslin, if the item will be lined.

You need to cover the layer of batting on the back with the lining or muslin before quilting so that it moves freely and doesn't catch on the machine.

Threads for machine quilting

As with other types of quilting, the thread you choose should relate to the qualities of your fabric. For quilting cotton, use cotton or polyester thread; for quilting silk, use silk, polyester, or embroidery threads.

Rayon has a wonderful sheen but breaks easily – so loosen the top tension of your machine.

Metallic-covered polyester threads will give your quilting a wonderful ritzy effect, but they must have a smooth surface to travel through the top tension of the machine easily. Experiment carefully with the fabric and stitch patterns that you will be using to find the best combinations.

Preparing your sewing machine

Needle sizes 70–80 are best for general "all-over" embroidery. If you are sewing silk or some polyester fabrics you will need a ballpoint needle. Check that the thread passes easily through the eye of the needle without shredding.

Keep a loose top tension (somewhere around three) and use a fancy stitch foot – if you use the zigzag foot you lose the dual feed facility.

Certain stitch keys are particularly useful. For example: the single pattern key, which completes a pattern and finishes; the pattern mirror key, which reverses a pattern to a mirror image; and the pattern start key, which returns a pattern being stitched to the stitching start point.

Preparing the fabrics

For garments, cut rectangles of fabric big enough to contain each pattern piece with a margin all around to allow for the slight shrinkage of the fabric that happens when it is quilted.

As with other methods of quilting, prepare the layers by basting the top fabric, batting, and backing fabric together with a grid of basting lines.

Baste around the outline of each pattern piece to give yourself a clear indication of your key pattern areas, but always embroider beyond the basting line so that the stitching goes right into the seams and will not unravel over time.

Stitches

Anything goes!

You will probably find it useful to work some samples on spare bits of fabric first of all, experimenting with different threads, stitch patterns, and pattern arrangements. To create interesting designs, vary the combinations, proximity, and thread colors of different stitch programs. You can work the patterns vertically, horizontally, or at random; you can move the fabric around as you stitch to give curves, wiggles, and wide sweeps.

The same combination of stitch programs was used on each of these samples. The pattern is a mirror image, with the wide Greek key pattern in the center, and some of the stitch patterns have been combined to form wider patterns.

The respective widths in millimetres of the stitch patterns, from left to right, are: 9, 12, 9,* 30,* 12, 38, 12,* 30,* 9, 12, 9 (the stars mark the gaps of unsewn fabric between patterns).

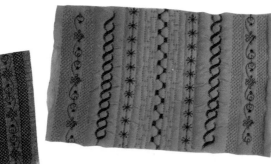

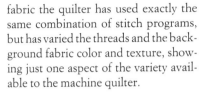

The finished jerkin. The quilter has stitched the pieces in the fuchsia silk with the fuchsia thread combination and carefully positioned the lines of quilting on the pattern pieces so that the fronts are exact reflections of each other. The jerkin has been lined and backed with the same fuchsia fabric and finished with fake pocket tops (stitched on flat fabric in one of the patterns used for the quilting) and covered buttons.

If you are working rows of patterns in one direction, you may find it useful to rule out (on graph paper if possible) the measurements of the different stitch patterns. You can then plan the gaps between them and work out where to position them on your project. This is especially important if you are making a garment, when you want the main areas of fancy stitching to be on the main areas of the pattern pieces, not hidden in a seam somewhere.

The gaps between the lines of stitching take on a shape of their own, and you will want to bear this in mind when you are trying out stitch combinations.

Quilt the fabric in ways that complement the final pattern if you are working on a garment. For example, quilt jackets and vests in vertical lines so that they don't look bulky, and avoid large strong patterns at bust level, for obvious reasons. Remember, too, that garments will have to be worn with other items of clothing, so the most colorful, complex designs don't always work the best – simple, rhythmic patterns work well, in themselves and with other patterns.

The samples shown below were all stitched as trial pieces for the pink bolero shown left. On each piece of fabric the quilter has used exactly the same combination of stitch programs, but has varied the threads and the background fabric color and texture, showing just one aspect of the variety available to the machine quilter.

Cutting the pattern pieces

Once your quilting is complete, lay the pattern pieces on the top and cut around them (you will probably find that you are cutting slightly outside your original basting because the quilting has pulled the fabric up slightly). Remember to match the patterns of the quilting as closely as possible. It is perfectly possible, if you are making something like a jacket and want the fronts or sleeves to match, to quilt large pieces of fabric first and then cut the pattern pieces from it afterward. Or you can quilt two pieces of fabric with the pattern going from right to left on one and from left to right on the other, then lay them right sides together after quilting, matching the patterns carefully, and cut out your pattern pieces. Alternatively, you may decide to make a completely asymmetric design, which can be very dramatic.

The fabrics and threads used here are: pink silk with pink and silver threads; blue cotton chambray with royal blue thread; painted pink silk with pink and dark silver threads; fuchsia silk with fuchsia thread; and painted blue/green silk, shaded from light to dark, with jade thread.

DESIGNING BY SEWING MACHINE

*I*NSPIRATION

Sewing machines make wonderful design partners for quilters; you can use them to create a patchwork fabric which you then quilt by hand, or to produce different kinds of quilting on all kinds of fabrics. All of the examples shown on these pages have made use of machine stitching for some of the piecing or quilting.

These two spectacular hats were made from machine-pieced patchwork pieces, which were then cut up and reassembled into the basic hat shapes. The patchwork has been stitched in regular lines of machine quilting which follow the contours of the hats.

The hat above is assembled from machine-pieced patchwork, and a quilted leaf has been stitched by machine, wired for strength and flexibility, and then appliquéd by hand to the finished article.

Many different fabrics, both printed and solid-colored, have been used in this quilt, called Reliquaries II. *The designer used a sewing machine to piece many of the sections, and also to quilt the finished panel in various places.*

168

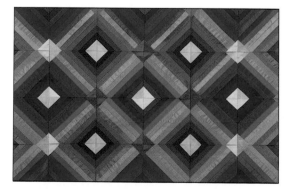

Symi I is a modern interpretation of a traditional Amish strip-piecing pattern. Printed and solid-colored fabrics in shades of blue have been strip-pieced by machine, then cut into triangles and stitched to solid triangles in shades of orange, with the shapes arranged so that the tones vary across the quilt.

The patchwork used in the panel above, Puer in Tenebris, is a mixture of machine strip-piecing and crazy patchwork; the fabrics have been joined in strips of varying widths, then cut and reassembled at different angles into squares. The final picture has been quilted by hand in different areas, using different colored threads and sewing beads into some of the quilting lines.

Symi IV uses another variation of strip-piecing. Solid fabrics have been machine pieced, then cut into squares, and reassembled so that the lines of strip-piecing form colored diamonds.

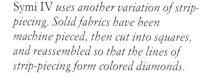

PATTERNS

Here is a range of patterns that can be used with many of the techniques shown in this book. Use them as they are or adapt them to suit your own taste and the design of the item you are making.

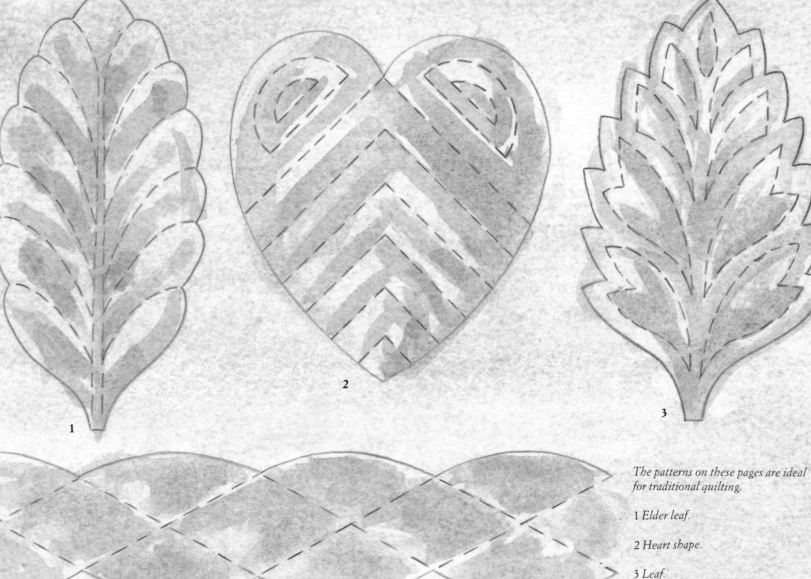

The patterns on these pages are ideal for traditional quilting.

1 Elder leaf.

2 Heart shape.

3 Leaf.

4 Twist border.

5 & 6 *Shells.*

7 *Fan corner.*

8 *Amish feather pattern.*

9 *Honeysuckle leaf.*

5

6

7

8

9

Traditionally associated with quilts, block patterns have imaginative and evocative names.

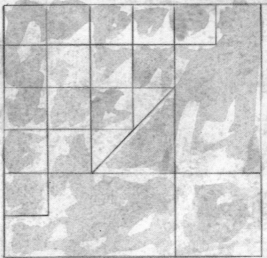

1 *Steps To The Altar.*

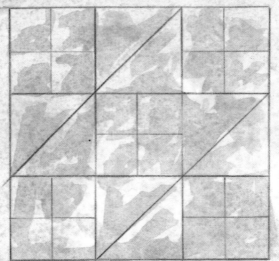

2 *Jacob's Ladder.*

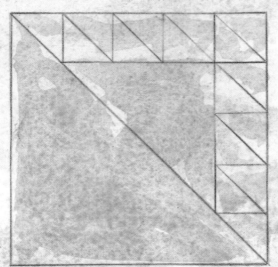

3 *Sawtooth.*

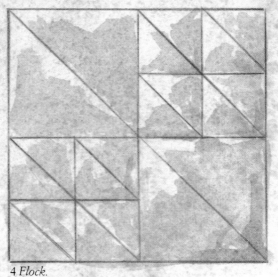

4 *Flock.*

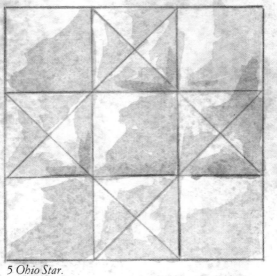

5 *Ohio Star.*

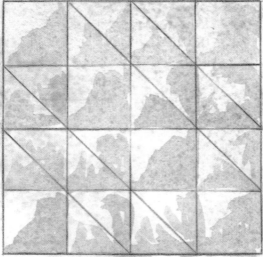

6 *Hovering Hawks.*

7 *Card Trick.*

8 *Milky Way.*

9 *Corn and Beans.*

This selection of geometric patterns is well suited to Sashiko quilting but can be used in many different quilting techniques.

CREDITS

The author would like to acknowledge and thank the originators of the projects featured in this book, those who made them, the manufacturers of products used and the photographers who produced such excellent work.

CHAPTER 1
Crib Quilt – Gail Lawther.
Placemats – designed by Gail Lawther, quilted by Gail Lawther and Rachel McIntyre.
Inspiration
Dragon Jerkin, Anita Faithfull; *Bow, Striped Cushion, Christmas Wreath*, Gail Lawther; *Top Cushion*, Eve May.

CHAPTER 2
Nautilus Tea Cozy – designed by Gail Lawther, quilted by Rachel McIntyre.
Classic Pillow Covers – Elaine Hammond.
Inspiration
White Quilt, Amish Design Quilt, Evelyne Wheeler; *Tulip Quilt*, Deirdre Amsden; *Swallow Jacket*, Joyce Hurren; *Persian Bath Mat*, photographed by Julia Hedgecoe, copyright Embroiderers' Guild Collection, Hampton Court Palace, England.

CHAPTER 3
Greeting Cards – Gail Lawther.
Water-lily Curtain – designed by Gail Lawther, quilted by Rachel McIntyre.
Inspiration
Samples, Heart, Bird, Fruit Bowl, Gail Lawther; *Textile Piece With Rice*, Rachele Verrecchia.

CHAPTER 4
Mirror Frame – Gail Lawther.
Clutch Purse – Anita Faithfull.
Inspiration
Reversible Jerkin, Evelyne Wheeler; *Make-up Bags, Palm Branch*, Gail Lawther; *Evening Jacket, Vermicelli Bag*, Anita Faithfull.

CHAPTER 5
Baby's Jacket – Ally Smith.
Baby's Coverlet – Ally Smith.
Inspiration
Textile Piece I, Textile Piece II, Tish Warrilow; *Pillow*, Eve May; *Samples*, Gail Lawther; *Singapore Orchids*, Isabel Dibden Wright; *Scrap Attack*, Joleen Mahoney Roe.

CHAPTER 6
Box Top – designed by Gail Lawther, quilted by Rachel McIntyre.
Rose Picture – Gail Lawther, inspired by a design by Ed Sibbett, Jr.
Rainbow Cushion Cover – Gail Lawther.
Inspiration
Orange Quilt, Evelyne Wheeler; *Tulips*, Isabel Dibden Wright; *Burnt Stones*, Helen Parrott.

CHAPTER 7
Nightgown Case – Gail Lawther.
Bright Rug – Gail Lawther.
Play Mat – Ally Smith.
Stained Glass Quilt – Gail Lawther.
Inspiration
Green Apples Jacket, Angela Besley; *Under the Shadow of His Wings, Galaxy I*, Gail Lawther; *Fleurs-de-Lys*, from the collection of the Museum of English Naive Art, The Countess Huntingdon Chapel, The Vineyard/Paragon, Bath, similar quilts available for sale from the Crane Gallery, London, England; *The Lord of the Dance*, Elizabeth Paine; *Red, Green, and White Quilt*, Beamish, The North of England Open Air Museum, County Durham; *Rose Window Quilt*, Angela Besley.

CHAPTER 8
Christmas Tree – Gail Lawther.
Striped Jerkin – Gail Lawther.
Shoulder Bag – Gail Lawther.
Fan Pillow Cover – Angela Besley.
Rainbow Fans Quilt – Angela Besley.
Inspiration
Sawtooth Quilt, from the collection of the Museum of English Naive Art, The Countess Huntingdon Chapel, The Vineyard/Paragon, Bath, similar quilts available for sale from the Crane Gallery, London, England; *Myomi*, Sylvia Williams; *Colorwash Stripe III*, Deirdre Amsden; *Isocomb*, Irene MacWilliam; *Basket Motif Quilt*, Beamish, The North of England Open Air Museum, County Durham; *Double Wedding Ring*, Angela Besley.

CHAPTER 9
Sewing Caddy – designed by Gail Lawther, quilted by Rachel McIntyre.
Album Cover – Gail Lawther.
Chinese Headboard – Gail Lawther.
Inspiration
Italian Corded Quilt, The Ulster Folk and Transport Museum; *Rouleau Piece*, Gail Lawther; *Experimental Piece*, Elizabeth Brimlow; *Panel, Pillow*, Gail Lawther.

CHAPTER 10
Tray Cloth – designed by Gail Lawther, quilted by Rachel McIntyre.
Spring Wallhanging – Gail Lawther.
Inspiration
Kamon I, Janice Gunner; *Cuffs, Cushion, Bags*, Margaret Blakeley; *Wallhanging with Flower Motif*, Evelyne Wheeler.

DESIGNING YOUR OWN QUILT
Pink Jerkin – Sandra Hurll.
Blues in the Night, Deirdre Amsden.
Inspiration
Hats, Evelyne Wheeler; *Reliquaries II, Puer in Tenebris*, Evelyn Montague; *Symi I, Symi IV*, Isabel Dibden Wright; *Hexagon Piece*, Gail Lawther.

Photograph of *Scrap Attack* on page 75 copyright of Joleen Mahoney Roe; all other photographs copyright of Quarto Publishing unless otherwise credited.

Machine embroidery and quilting threads supplied by Madeira Threads (U.K.) Ltd; stencil plastic supplied by Leicester Laminating Services.

Porcelain doll (Chapter 5) supplied by Pat Gardiner, Pretty Things, London.